AN
INDUSTRIAL COCKTAIL

Lord Haslam was born at Bolton in 1923, became captain of Bolton School, its cricket and football teams and, after graduating from Birmingham University with a first class mining degree, started work at Manchester Collieries, getting his Colliery Manager's Certificate. Disillusioned by promotion prospects, he was recruited by ICI's Nobel Division in 1947 to support UK and overseas customers using explosives in mining and other operations – the unexpected beginning of a brilliant global career spanning thirty-three years with Britain's biggest industrial company.

While the Division's personnel director, the 'Haslam Panel' devised the first pay scheme for all ICI posts up to middle manager; in Plastics Division he quadrupled polyester film output and became deputy chairman; Fibres Division returned to profit under his chairmanship. On the main board from 1974–83, he marshalled key people for leading posts as Personnel Director and was promoted to the top triumvirate of three deputy chairmen, responsible for all operations throughout the Americas.

Moving on to be chairman of Tate & Lyle and British Steel, he injected new ideas into these contrasting businesses. His five years as British Coal chairman up to 1990 were the pinnacle of his career and his biggest challenge – confirming that retrenching a major industry in a shrinking market is far more difficult than expanding a business in a growth market. On the Court of the Bank of England from 1985–93, he felt the threat of inflation was consistently overstated; as an advisory director of Unilever PLC around the same time, he headed up its first audit committee. In semi-retirement he was chairman of Bechtel Ltd, which took over construction management of London's faltering Jubilee Line, and also Wasserstein Perella, where his last act was to introduce Wal-Mart to the UK. His wife Joyce died from cancer in 1995.

He was active in education, industrial health and charities as chairman of Manchester Business School council, Bolton school governors and the national children's welfare charity The Michael Sieff Foundation, founded by his second wife Elizabeth.

Knighted and made a Freeman of the City of London in 1985 and created a life peer in 1990, Lord Haslam died, also from cancer, on 2 November 2002 aged 79.

AN
INDUSTRIAL COCKTAIL

BOB HASLAM

ROBERT HALE · LONDON

ISBN 0 7090 7059 4

Robert Hale Limited
Clerkenwell House
Clerkenwell Green
London EC1R 0HT

A catalogue record for this book is available from the British Library

2 4 6 8 10 9 7 5 3 1

Typeset by Derek Doyle & Associates, Liverpool
Printed in Great Britain by
St Edmundsbury Press Limited, Bury St Edmunds,
and bound by
Woolnough Bookbinding Limited, Irthlingborough

Contents

Preface by
Lady Elizabeth Haslam

As he was happily winding down after a long and brilliant career at the helm of key global industries and having led a cluster of good causes, Bob set himself an objective which was foremost in his mind. He was determined to finish this book of his life.

Sadly, after the remission of five enjoyable years, the cancer which he seemed to have conquered flared up in the lymphatic system and intensive chemotherapy and radiotherapy were only able to check rather than cure it. He died peacefully with his family around him on 2 November 2002, barely three months before becoming an octogenerian, but knowing that his book, which he called from the beginning *An Industrial Cocktail*, was virtually complete.

The book was Bob's eager preoccupation in the latter period of the twenty years since we first met and our all too short six happy years of married life together. While remaining deeply involved in the business of the House of Lords, Select Committees and other causes, he blocked out in his diary most days of the week to work on the book, marshalling information about a multitude of people, events and decisions as well as double-checking for accuracy. It was demanding but not too difficult because he was a methodical man, having saved significant press cuttings, letters, photographs and, of course, diaries – all in easy-to-find date order.

'What do you think of this?' he would ask, showing me a section or a chapter when particularly pleased about his writing. If there was something I couldn't understand, he always wanted to make it clear, though I must say my own input was quite modest. Having regarded too many books about industry as more like fiction than fact – particularly Ian MacGregor's on the coal industry – Bob was eager to get at the truth, to set the record straight. He also wanted it to be an amusing and entertaining read and humour often does shine through. He had a mine of wonderful stories and, although I have heard many before, it is still a joy to read them in context.

In passing the book for press, Bob would have expressed heartfelt thanks to all friends and colleagues who gave him guidance, ideas and comments – whether or not he felt able to take them all on board. He would also have been impressed by the permissions readily given to reproduce book texts and illustrations. When the book was just an idea, he was grateful for the encouragement given by Geoffrey Goodman – whose perceptive press and broadcasting interviews over the years he valued – also for helping to shape the introductory guidelines and for his subsequent support. As the venture was getting underway, he keenly welcomed the close involvement of Norman Woodhouse whose subsequent searching discussions, diligent research, steering on style and piloting to publication have been invaluable. He would have been delighted by the ready agreement – despite so many other commitments – of his long-standing friend Joel Barnett to write a Foreword. This book would not even be ready for publication without the skills, patience and perseverance of Bob's secretary, Marjorie Arnell, who prepared and corrected all the manuscripts and made so many helpful suggestions. Nor would it have gone to press without the positive and professional involvement of John Hale and his team.

I was determined to fulfil one of Bob's last wishes as my priority and – thanks to the devoted efforts of those around us – this has been achieved admirably with the posthumous publication of An Industrial Cocktail.

Foreword by The Rt. Hon. the Lord (Joel) Barnett PC

I am grateful for the opportunity to pay a personal tribute to a man about whom it can be truly said, the word 'distinguished' is a huge understatement! Some of the better obituaries gave a glimpse of his tremendous contribution to industrial and public life. This book spells out his quite fascinating career from 1947 when he joined ICI, through to his chairmanship of British Steel, British Coal and then back again to the private sector as chairman of a number of major companies. Even in what he calls his 'semi-retirement' (1994–2000) he had, as he puts it, a 'rewarding involvement' as Chairman of the newly formed British Occupational Health Research Foundation.

I first met Robert when I was Chief Secretary to the Treasury from 1974 to 1979 but we really became close friends when he came to the House of Lords, in particular when he joined the Select Committee on European Trade and Industry Affairs which I chaired at the time. It was a personal pleasure for me, but more importantly, he soon made his own contribution to the reports we produced.

We were in opposing political parties, but this made no difference to what I believe was a wonderful friendship. It certainly helped that we both came from the North-west, he from Bolton, round the corner, as it were, from Manchester where I was born. I also read with special interest that his family moved to a semi-detached house when he was four years old. My own family moved to a similar house when I was three!

Although we may have been in different political parties, as his book spells out we shared strong views on many important issues of the day. In particular, the question of whether the UK should join the euro. Despite being a loyal member of the Conservative Party, he strongly disagreed with their policy, and expressed his clear view that it was in the national interest that we should join. There were of course many who disagreed, but they would never doubt his sincerity, and would have to respect the strength of his arguments. I certainly share his views on the five tests the Chancellor, Gordon Brown, has laid down as having to be met before we could consider it would be right on economic grounds to recommend a 'Yes' vote in a referendum. It was clear to both of us that economic convergence could never be sustainable as the Chancellor's tests required. Indeed we questioned the whole issue of a referendum to decide so complex an economic issue. I would never dispute the democratic right of the average man or woman in the street to decide how, and by whom, we should be governed, but I do doubt whether there will be many who could understand whether sustainable economic convergence has been met! Indeed, Gordon Brown himself could not guarantee it. This book reinforces my personal sadness that Bob Haslam's powerful views will not be heard on this, as on many other important issues.

There is another major question that the book discusses which has become of great concern. I refer to the work of non-executive directors, with especial reference to their membership of audit committees. The way these committees were constituted, and how they worked (or did not work!), blew up with some force in the Enron case in the United States, with the notable UK interest involving the major political figure of Lord Wakeham, who was both a non-executive director and a member of the audit committee. Along with others, he is now in danger of being faced with substantial claims by shareholders who will have lost fortunes through Enron's use of off-balance sheet partnerships, with apparently huge hidden liabilities. In this book, Bob refers to his experience as a non-executive director of a large multinational company, Unilever, and he writes about his work as Chairman of the Audit Committee. He says the committee was 'ably' served by the auditors, Coopers and Lybrand (since merged to be one of the internationally recognized 'big four' – it was 'five' until Anderson dropped out). I have no doubt that was true, but the Enron affair, and the alleged collusion between the Chairman, the Finance Director and a senior partner of such a large and highly respected firm as Anderson, raises new issues. One doubts if even a man of Bob's calibre and industrial experience would have been able to detect that type of fraud. We must hope that new methods of separating the internal audit system from external auditors and the appointment of non-executive directors other than simply cronies or friends of the chairman, will ensure that men or women like Bob Haslam will be around to prevent another Enron!

The book also refers to another issue of current international concern, what Bob describes as the hazards of nuclear power stations. The world-wide threats from terrorists have underlined the concerns that particularly troubled Bob. His great experience in energy led him to express concern, not only about nuclear power and the terrorist threat, but about the serious potential problem of the growing number of power stations dominated by gas, where he foresaw the UK having to import up to 90 per cent by the year 2020. That he felt would be a 'proverbial tea party' compared to other problems facing the UK. He wonders what is being done. One hopes that at the very least, this book will remind ministers that urgent action is required.

The same could also be said about the other regularly expressed concern, global warming! Western countries, apart from the United States, have signed up to what is known as the Kyoto Agreement, but in practice, as Bob gently points out, most simply pay lip service to it.

It should be emphasized that this excellent book, while based on his wide experience of serious errors made by many senior ministers and officials, makes no personal or political criticism, but rather exposes serious mistakes made in crucial public areas. It fulfils a great need for positive action on subjects where his experience commands respect.

Bob Haslam had an independent mind. As one obituary rightly put it, he was a managerial giant. His book should be read by all who care about what the title, *An Industrial Cocktail*, signifies. That is the experience of an intelligent man's actual work in a large number of fields vital to the national interest.

Illustrations

Between pages 64 and 65

Picture Credits

Jeff Poar/Yorkshire Regional Photographic Department, British Coal: 15.
Yorkshire Regional Photographic Department, British Coal: 16. uppa.co.uk: 24.
Ron McTrusty/*Engineer*: 28 & 29. Richard Willson/*TheTimes*: 30.

Every effort has been made to obtain the consent of the copyright holders and the publishers regret any omissions.

Introduction

I am writing this book because I believe that my generation of industrialists/managers has something significant to tell contemporary society. I come from a generation that in the twentieth century has seen more social, economic, technological and, arguably, political change, than any other previous century. The entire industrial world has been turned upside down. We are now involved in a technological revolution as significant and as momentous as the first industrial revolution. But that does not mean the lessons learned by my generation can be forgotten, ignored or dismissed as irrelevant. Far from it. In my view modern industrial/commercial management, as well as political leaders, can learn from our failures as well as our modest successes. This is what I hope will emerge from my story.

The former industrial tycoons are oft-times now described as 'yesteryear's men' (and of course they *were* mostly men) who shaped Britain's economic life in the post-war years – that is the period from 1945 until Margaret Thatcher became Prime Minister. Of course they were inevitably a mixed bunch – some very good, even outstanding by world standards, others poor and, in some instances, frankly inadequate. They were also frequently misjudged, often misunderstood. The world changed slowly to start with and then, some time in the early 1960s, there was an explosion which can perhaps only now be seen in a more rational perspective. Much of what was happening and changing at that time was simply not understood sufficiently by anyone – management, trade unions, academics, politicians, church leaders, governments. Everything was changing too quickly. Perhaps it still is.

What I have tried to do in this book is to explain what we did, what I did, against that background. And because I emerged from a background that was typical of the working class, I believe I was able to view my experiences in a different light from many others in my spheres of activity.

It was, as I have described it, an 'industrial cocktail'. It was shaken together from disparate, fruitful and enjoyable concoctions, to be imbibed slowly with pauses. Try it for taste. . . .

1
The Early Days

My cocktail has been well stirred, has many flavours and was changed by a variety of unexpected and unusual ingredients.

The story starts in 1923 in Bolton, Lancashire, when I was born in a 'Coronation Street'-type terraced house.

From a small shop my father, Percy, and his two brothers ran a painting and decorating business inherited from my grandfather. Father was out working nearly every day and one of my earliest memories is at the age of four helping to push along cobbled streets a handcart full of paint, planks and ladders for his next job. Even the wheels were bigger than me so I could not have been much help but, typical of my father's encouragement, he gave everyone the impression I was doing a useful job.

Mother – Mary-Alice, but called Cissy – always referred to my father as a 'master painter' and he certainly took pride in doing a good job. Before my birth, mother was a 'little piecer' in a cotton mill. Her work involved joining up the spindles and she lost part of a finger in an accident, but she got on with life without complaining and never regarded it as a handicap.

When I was four years old we moved to a semi-detached house with a garden and, for the first time, a room with a bath and lavatory, which seemed the ultimate form of luxury. It was also a relief for me because our previous loo was in the backyard where I spent many anxious minutes, which seemed like hours, waiting for my grandfather to finish his smoke, read his newspaper and only then emerge from his favourite retreat. Even after moving, my mother still had to do her laundry in an outdoor wash-house and after school every Monday afternoon it was my job to turn the handle on the mangle for her.

My family were strong Methodists. My other grandfather, who died before I was born and was one of fourteen children, was a lay preacher and always cycled to wherever he was preaching, as he would not use public transport on Sundays. My grandmother, too, would not draw water or use electricity on Sundays, as it involved other people working on the Sabbath. My parents followed this same pattern of behaviour, but not quite so vigorously. Indeed my father usually found an excuse on Sundays to visit his sister, who was married to a headmaster and lived nearby, and I soon discovered the main attraction – he wanted to read their Sunday paper!

I was taken to Chalfont Street Independent Methodist Church twice each Sunday, walking a mile each way because my father also would not use public transport. It was a long slog for a lad and uncomfortable in winter, but for me it was a family routine. My father, who was Church Secretary, took me to morning Sunday school and my mother joined us at the evening service, but the sermons were above my head at the time. Church bazaars were more interesting because I helped my mother to sell bric-à-brac.

Early holidays were at Blackpool and Llandudno, and at the age of seven we participated in holidays organized by the Methodists at Ilfracombe, Clacton and Scarborough. Unlike at home, there were prayers every day. I was often the only child in the group so my parents encouraged me to respond to adults. That sort of holiday would not appeal to many boys nowadays but I used to enjoy it, ticking off the weeks until the next break. I greatly treasure a photograph of my father on a sunny Scarborough beach, unseasonally dressed in his Sunday best, complete with bowler hat, and my motorboat tucked under his arm!

As an only child, I was spoilt by my parents, though not to the extent of getting my own way. They were devoted to my well-being and this devotion was sustained throughout their lives. I cannot remember ever being slapped by them; any disciplining was done verbally, talking things through, rather than physically. If someone came to the door and my mother felt I had been abrupt, she would tell me the polite way of dealing with people. Two of my young cousins were like brothers and were always around, so I was never lonely. I liked the outdoors and nothing pleased us more than camping out in the garden or playing our style of football and cricket with other children on a nearby rough patch of ground.

Standing at the garden gate most mornings, my mother would wave me off to Church Road Council School and, in the afternoon, she was there to welcome me home. From the age of five I spent six happy years at the school, preferring games to classroom work and – not being a book addict – reading only the set pieces. My parents were pleased when I became head boy at the age of eleven but, looking back, it was not a demanding role, with tasks like standing in front of the school to say a few words, setting an example in the playground and stopping fellow pupils misbehaving, though there was virtually no bullying in those days.

Following a bad attack of bronchitis during the Second World War my father was not a well man but he encouraged me to take part in all sports. Whenever I played football or cricket for the school he came to watch the whole match, sometimes being the only parent there. I could tell by the expression on his face if I had done something daft or praiseworthy. He took me to Bolton Wanderers matches even on Christmas Day – much against his normal Christian beliefs. I can vividly picture the scene at the end of the match when men in the posh stand opposite lit up their Christmas cigars which glowed in the twilight, like swarms of darting fireflies.

Bolton School was *the* school to go to and at the age of eleven I knew I wanted to be there. My parents had always had that ambition, but my father could not afford the fees. I took a scholarship examination, sitting in the ornate Great Hall, but was not successful. The Headmaster, Richard Poskitt, however, wrote that he would like to see me in the school and came to an arrangement by which my father would pay only half the fee. This was the first important turning point in my life, and I shall always owe a great debt to my late Headmaster, who inspired me throughout my schooling.

I progressed with a fairly average academic performance, playing a lot of games and swimming in the indoor pool most afternoons before returning home at 5 p.m. to do some homework. On joining, I regarded the school captain as a god-like character and never dreamed I might assume this role. However, I became School Captain of the boys' division and captain of the football and cricket elevens – a source of great pride to my parents. For me it was a sporting pinnacle. At football I was centre-half most of the time, mainly defending and not scoring too many goals. At cricket, bowling was my particular forte, but eventually I developed into an all-rounder.

The period 1940/1, when I was School Captain, was unusually exciting and demanding. As most young masters had been called up for war service, some forms had young women teachers, who sometimes found it difficult to exert discipline among boys only a few years younger. With other monitors I was called on to restore order in the form rooms and the playground, without too much difficulty because there was a general respect for the authority of the monitors. Unlike today, there were few real troublemakers and no drugs problem. I rarely found it necessary to inflict the mandatory hundred lines on a young offender.

There was a strict dividing line – almost a Berlin Wall – between the separate boys' and girls' divisions. We were never allowed to get together at school though, as monitors with our own room, we could see the girls getting on and off the trams. We all had our favourites by sight, though I never had a special heart-throb.

Boy sixth-formers were responsible for fire-watching for both divisions, getting to know the walkways criss-crossing the roofs to deal with any hostile incendiary bombs and sleeping on the premises on a rota basis. The girls' contribution was to prepare our emergency rations, which were usually rock buns and were indeed well-named. Bolton was not a prime target for German bombers, but when Manchester or Liverpool were being attacked, the air-raid sirens sounded and we positioned ourselves on top of the central tower – imposingly designed as a replica of Hampton Court. Only the occasional bomb or incendiary fell in the Bolton area and thankfully none on the school, though local fire-watchers from nearby roads came to shelter under the tower archway. We used to relieve the monotony by trying to hit the helmets of our fellow fire-watchers down below with our liberal supply of rock buns. If successful, a helmet would ring, as though hit by a piece of shrapnel! The Headmaster joined us from time to time and even participated in our escapades.

One morning I was summoned to the Headmaster's room to be confronted by Miss Varley, the formidable Headmistress of the girls' division, who was fuming. She wagged a finger at me and said: 'Do you know your boys have found a way of secretly meeting my girls? Not only that – they are actually smoking together. You must find the culprits!' She ranted on and left to hand out punishment to her miscreant girls. Indeed, the central boiler which heated both schools was alongside the locker room where we slept when fire-watching. Some daring lads had discovered an underground walkway along the pipeline leading to the girls' division and this was the secret daytime meeting place. 'You should try to find out who's doing it – but don't try too hard,' was the Headmaster's discreet advice to me.

Richard Poskitt was a strong character and he had a formidable reputation with parents, but I got to know him well as School Captain and discovered his warm, human side. He joined in some of the fun at school and agricultural camps, when we did our bit to help the farmers' war effort. With his family evacuated to the Lake District he was quite a lonely man, and invited me to go to the cinema with him from time to time.

I took it in turn with other monitors to read the lesson at school prayers every morning and if any failed to appear I had to step in at short notice, though I was not the most accomplished of readers. For some strange reason I was always called Sam at school, maybe because there was an earlier Bob Haslam. Standing in for an absent monitor one morning, I stood at the lectern with no idea of the lesson until I started to read the lines: 'The Lord came and stood there and called Samuel, Samuel. Samuel answered "Speak; thy servant hears thee".' The whole school, including masters, erupted into laughter. In later years, when an apparent stranger would stop me in London with the greeting 'Hello Sam!', I knew instinctively that we had been together at Bolton School.

Our Christmas carol service, fashioned on the one at King's College,

Cambridge, was an unforgettable experience in the Great Hall for the thousand-strong congregation, including my parents who were brimming over with pride when I read a lesson.

The only subject for which I seemed to have some flair was geography, taught by 'Pip' Porter, an inspirational teacher. In 1941 I had an Open Scholarship to read geography at Cambridge, but unfortunately failed the entrance examination in Latin, which I wrongly believed had been abandoned because of the war. It meant mocking up the equivalent of School Certificate Latin in just a few weeks. Everyone told me it was virtually impossible not to pass, but I did the impossible with flying colours! Perversely the Latin requirement was abandoned the following year.

As Cambridge was out, the Headmaster said I should establish myself for a year at another university before being called up, so I applied to Birmingham to read geography. However, before arriving the Registrar wrote that they were phasing out the geography school temporarily because of the war and asked if I would like to read geology. This opportunity was also short-lived as the geology school followed the same fate as geography. The suggestion was now of a coal mining degree, which contained a lot of geology.

By then I really could not have cared less what degree I took, particularly as I had enlisted into the 'Y Scheme', which would have led me into the Navy in a year's time. However, by the time I appeared before the Joint Recruiting Board, coal mining had become a highly reserved occupation and I was told the Navy was not for me. This led to me qualifying as a mining engineer. Failing that Latin examination at Cambridge was undoubtedly the second unplanned turning point in my life and looking back I have never regretted it.

Years later I was to discover a family link with mining. Research about me for a Granada TV programme revealed that my great grandfather had worked as a coal miner in Lancashire some 150 years before. His marriage certificate indicated that both he and his wife were totally illiterate, each having signed the register with a cross.

Leaving home for the first time and waving farewell to my tearful mother was an emotional moment. I knew she would have preferred me to head in a different direction, perhaps becoming geography master at Bolton School. My father was content with my choice, being determined that I should not follow him in the family decorating business. He was an intelligent and able man and a university education would have led to a fine career, but as it was he tended to relive his life through me.

Life at Birmingham University in wartime was understandably much more rigorous than normal and I soon became absorbed in it. We had to complete a four-year mining engineering course in three, carry out regular fire-watching duties and do military training in the Engineering Corps of the Officer Cadet Corps.

In my second year I became Secretary of the Guild of Undergraduates, as the students' union was called. We were responsible for the management of the union buildings and the organization of a wide range of student activities and many other tasks. In my final year I was voted in as President, and it was my first real management role. With competitors standing against me for the post, it helped that I was well known among groups of students for both my guild and sporting activities.

All student leisure activities revolved around the union. Ours were mainly run-of-the-mill management actions rather than policy decisions – something like running a conference centre-cum-hotel. With no worldly experience between us, it was seat-of-the-pants stuff – arranging meetings of all kinds, inviting politicians to speak, fixing bar opening and shutting times and rents for letting rooms. Nevertheless it involved managing a group of people, with the added challenge of maintaining standards despite wartime restrictions, including such complications as, for example, who was to clean the men's loos as there were no longer any male staff available. Throughout my time we had to expel only three or four students from the union for serious financial misdeeds.

Inevitably there were some abnormal challenges. For example, the National Union of Students had commendably asked all university unions to make available visiting facilities for any former union members who were young officers serving in the forces nearby. Most took up the invitation by joining our Saturday dances and this predictably tended to heighten the level of sexual activity. The

Birmingham newspapers undoubtedly exaggerated the problem but one Monday I was summoned by our distinguished Vice-Chancellor, Sir Raymond Priestley, to explain our shortcomings in managing discipline in the union.

It was not a sex orgy or anything like that, but some of the visitors arrived at our dances with local girls and, unseen by any of our marshals, slipped away to find an empty room. I assured the Vice-Chancellor we were taking all possible action, but it had to be limited to measures like locking all doors and patrolling the corridors. I explained there was little chance of taking disciplinary action against even the few people caught, because the men came from other universities and the girls from the locality. Fortunately the headlines did not persist. Altogether, it was a valuable baptism into management and I was fortunate to be surrounded by some extremely able colleagues, from whom I learned a great deal.

I was also Captain of the university football team, but because of wartime conditions we played primarily against local teams. One Saturday we beat an Army XI 10–0. The next weekend we were playing an RAF XI, but for security reasons we were never informed about the visiting team's players. Imagine my surprise when the first man off their bus was Stanley Matthews, followed by Raich Carter. I was playing centre-half that day and three times Matthews passed with such precision that Carter, with his back to me, kicked the ball over his shoulder into the net, leaving me totally helpless. They won 7–1. Such were the ups and downs of university football in those times! Another highlight was being selected for English Universities against Scottish Universities on Aston Villa's ground – incidentally with two other ex-Bolton School boys in our team: Norman Tate and Harry Whittle.

Our shorter vacations were taken up fully with work experience and military training. On an earlier career visit as a Bolton schoolboy I had been aghast at the coalface conditions in a nearby Lancashire small mine. It seemed incredible that anyone could work a coal seam deep underground only 3 feet high and I said to a friend at the time: 'There's no way I'm going to get involved in anything like this.' However, most of my vacations were spent underground at Chanters Colliery in

Atherton, which looked like a palace compared with my earlier fleeting experience. I met Humphrey Browne, then Managing Director of Manchester Collieries, who was to have an important influence on my early mining career. He offered me a university scholarship, which I foolishly declined as I felt it would put me under too much of an obligation.

I also spent one vacation working at Geevor tin mine in Cornwall, staying at a cottage in Pendeen Village where my landlady provided a splendid Cornish pasty for my underground snack and varied its contents every day. I found tin mining even more rigorous and demanding than coal mining. There was added tension caused by occasional German air raids on Plymouth, which led to alerts in our part of Cornwall. We were then caught underground as the cages in the main shaft were not operational. We were allowed to climb the ladders in the shaft, but as this was an ascent of 1,000 feet or more, it was a real gamble whether to climb or wait for the 'all clear'. I twice made this arduous exit from underground and each time beat the 'all clear' siren.

Geevor mine is now a museum and a leisure centre and in 1998 the trustees asked me to open a new restaurant there. It was a nostalgic visit and I was impressed to see what an attractive and interesting location the site has become. I was very touched by an old miner who remembered me as a student, and who said I was the best dressed man he had ever seen down Geevor. He reminded me that on leaving I gave him my dirty suit, which he had thoroughly cleaned and wore it as his Sunday best!

My periods of military training were an interesting contrast. On a course at Clitheroe which focused on building Bailey bridges, I got my thumb jammed between two heavy sections and finished with my arm in a sling. The following weekend I was travelling by bus to visit my family in Bolton, ten days after the D-day landings and, despite my protestations, some of the ladies decided I must have been injured in action. They insisted on giving me some of their precious rations. It was one of the most embarrassing moments of my life and made me realize I was having a soft kind of war. I felt very humble.

I graduated with a first-class degree in 1944. I can only assume my papers had been marked in a sympathetic way, in recognition of my demanding role of Guild President and other diverse activities.

2

Manchester Collieries: 1944–7

My mining degree and vacation work inevitably led me to embark on a career in the coal industry. Manchester Collieries had a reputation as a progressive company, so I joined in July 1944, working initially at Gibfield Colliery, followed by Bedford and Mosley Common Collieries – all in Lancashire.

My life then was a combination of working, studying – one day a week at Wigan Technical College – and courting. To progress in the coal industry it was essential to get a Colliery Manager's Certificate which meant, even with a university degree, working three years underground, with eighteen months on the coal face. Having achieved these milestones I passed the examination in June 1947 and, at the age of twenty-four, married my first wife, Joyce, a few days later – quite a week!

Joyce had failed to get into the Women's Land Army in the Second World War because, like me, she was in a reserved occupation, working in De Havilland's aircraft factory. Ours was one of those low-key post-wartime weddings and my best man at St Paul's Church, Bolton, was Harry Whittle – a close friend since schooldays and an amazing athlete who led the British team at the Helsinki Olympics, the first after the war. Following our Torquay honeymoon, Joyce and I started married life living with my parents.

Working on the coal face was very demanding physically – a pick-and-shovel slog with mechanization still in its infancy. I often wondered, as a graduate, why I was there, but in retrospect it was one of the best things that ever happened to me. The camaraderie of the miners operating in this alien environment was great to see and I learned a lot about working relationships and motivation. It was probably worth ten times any work experience in other industrial settings.

The mining technique was to undercut the seam with a mechanical coal cutter, drill holes, insert explosives, and blast down the coal. Rigid steel supports, the thickness of the seam, were hammered in to support the roof but withdrawing them with a device called a Sylvester was always a tricky job, as the roof immediately collapsed behind.

When I was put in charge of an underground district, every Friday afternoon involved negotiating the pay packets for miners on piece-work. Their pay depended basically on how much coal they had produced or how many yards of tunnel they had driven. There were always claims for exceptional circumstances like excessive water on the coal face or hitting a heavily faulted area. Arguing about it with the miners' chargemen was all part of the culture. It was not unusual to spend a couple of hours arguing about a few shillings. When I walked into the local pub at night, however, I would be offered a double whisky by the same man, so there were no hard feelings!

Qualifying in mine rescue activities meant being trained to use all the rescue gear and oxygen equipment on a mock coal face. Having qualified, I joined on a 'call basis' a highly experienced cadre of people who were permanently available at the local rescue station. I was called out on only two emergencies following underground explosions, neither of which was a major incident.

On 1 January 1947, a date deeply etched in my memory, the National Coal Board flag was hoisted in the pit yard at Mosley Common Colliery to mark the brave new era of state ownership – a move that was supported with great enthusiasm by the hundreds of miners present. The mood was epitomized by the pit joiner standing next to me, who was responsible for maintaining wooden guides for the pit cages at his small, pit bottom workshop. He was rarely called into action and broke the monotony by his own version of private enter-prise – discreetly making garden gates, which he had to dismantle and surreptitiously smuggle out piece by piece. He turned to me with tears in his eyes and said: 'Now the pits are ours I'll never make another gate!' Nevertheless, the miners gave me a garden gate as a wedding present!

At that stage of the war, coal was tightly rationed and there was an unwritten understanding that miners could bring out each shift one large lump of coal for domestic use. It was quite a sight to see miners waddling from the pit shaft to the baths weighed down by the lump of coal in their shirts, like an army of penguins. Prominent in their midst was the pit joiner walking ramrod stiff like an army officer – with yet another piece of a gate hidden under his shirt and trousers!

'Bevin Boys' – men who were conscripted to work in the mines instead of serving in the forces – were employed in my sector at Mosley Common. One was Nat Lofthouse, who became one of the 'greats' of English football. His gruelling programme on Saturday match days was to go underground at 6 a.m., work a full shift, surface at 1 p.m. and board the team coach for one of the nearby First Division football grounds. I was delighted to meet Nat again more than fifty years later at the Reebok Stadium when he became President of Bolton Wanderers, the team I still support.

A memory I would rather forget is travelling in the mornings on the pit buses with miners who would happily have smoked two cigarettes and a pipe at the same time, knowing they could not have another puff for nine hours. The air was so bad I decided to take a gas sampling bottle from the pit in my overcoat pocket. That same morning I sent up a sample taken on the bus to the surface laboratory, along with those from my coal face. Two hours later the laboratory chief rang me excitedly and shouted: 'You must withdraw the men immediately. I am informing the Manager that the carbon dioxide and carbon monoxide concentrations in one bottle are way above the acceptable levels.' I urged him to pause a moment and see if the offending bottle had the letter 'B' on the label. He confirmed it had and I guiltily admitted that the miners' early morning bus was the source!

Humphrey Browne, Managing Director of Manchester Collieries, took a continuing interest in my development and indicated that, when I got my Colliery Manager's Certificate, I would become an assistant manager. But by then he had moved on to greater things, later becoming NCB Deputy Chairman. My new bosses came from Wigan Coal Corporation and there was a tradition of great rivalry between the two companies. Their views about my immediate future were much less palatable and I told them the night overman's job offered to me for the next two years was of no interest. That evening in the local pub a man sitting on the next bar stool summed up my mood. 'You look really fed up,' he said. I said I was and explained why. He worked for the Nobel Division, ICI's explosives business, and cheered me up by saying: 'We're looking for someone like you.'

Three days later I was interviewed in Glasgow and offered a job on the spot. On returning I tendered my resignation. My NCB bosses tried to keep me by reinstating the original offer of an assistant manager's job. Too late, I told them. I had already accepted the ICI post and it was my preferred option. I subsequently received a letter from Humphrey Browne expressing disappointment at this turn of events and asking me to let him know exactly why it had happened. I was sad to have to let him down, but this move to ICI in October 1947 became the third unplanned beneficial turning point in my early career.

3
ICI Nobel Division: 1947–61

It was an exciting career move when I joined the Technical Service Department of Nobel Division in Glasgow in October 1947, when ICI was Britain's largest industrial company. Our main role was to advise and support customers using explosives in deep and opencast mining, quarrying, oil prospecting and producing, civil engineering projects, all kinds of demolitions and many other applications.

Joyce and I acquired our first house in Glasgow and both our sons were to be born there. They subsequently became embarrassed to find that they had English parents!

John Garnet joined Nobel Division on the same day as me and we and our wives became good friends. One Sunday we were strolling together round the lake in our local park. Our wives were pushing Roger, our son, in his pram and John and I were following with their daughter, Virginia, in her pram. John suddenly took off to see a friend on the other side of the lake and I was left holding the proverbial baby! Needless to say she started to cry profusely, as she assumed her father had abandoned her with this strange man, of whom she clearly disapproved. Virginia was eventually to marry Peter Bottomley and have a distinguished political career, joining the Cabinet as Secretary of State for Health. I have had the pleasure on two occasions of introducing her at meetings and was able to say without fear of contradiction, 'I have known Virginia longer than anyone else in this room!' Her father, after an earlier career in ICI Personnel, was invited to become Chief

Executive of the Industrial Society, a role which almost seemed designed to meet his many talents, and which he performed to perfection.

One of my more dramatic jobs was designing and firing large quarry blasts, using tons of explosives. One memorable blast was at Ronez Point, Jersey. It took nearly a week to charge, but on the morning of the firing a notice in the *Jersey Weekly Post* informed shipping 'not to approach within one mile of Ronez Point today' – such was the local confidence in my calculations! All went well and over 100,000 tons of granite landed within 200 yards of the original face.

Most routine visits were to UK coal mines, including an unforgettable assignment in the Somerset coalfield, which then had six small mines where blasting was carried out using a safety fuse and plain detonators. I had the task of converting them to using electric detonators and delay detonators in tunnelling operations. Having finished one underground session around midnight, I surfaced to find the pithead baths locked until the following morning, so I decided to drive in my pit clothes to the upmarket Royal Crescent Hotel in Bath. When I walked through the entrance with a black face and carrying my pit helmet, the night porter obviously thought I was a 'loony' and would not give me my room key. Fortunately I knew the Manager lived in the hotel so he had his night's sleep disturbed to vouch for me and I finally returned wearily to my room. I had much the same problem in the restaurant early next morning getting the staff to serve breakfast to me in my pit overalls, and clearly my fellow guests were wondering what on earth I was doing there.

One of Glasgow's reputations was for criminals who specialized in blasting open safes with explosives. Occasionally the charges failed to explode and we were called in by the police to extract the residual explosive. At weekends this involved me being picked up at home by a police car, which certainly created the wrong impression with curious neighbours!

Another service was to advise customers on the potentially adverse vibrational effects of their blasting activities. One of our leading scientists, George Morris, had established a high reputation in this field and on one occasion we both visited an opencast coal site in Scotland,

where the owner of a landed house was complaining of extensive plaster cracking. George explained that according to his formula there was
no possibility of this being caused by the nearby blasting; however, we
would take a reading of a blast with his seismograph to prove it. I was
despatched to the opencast site to fire the blast and returned to find
George and the houseowner emerging from the front door covered in
plaster, as the lounge ceiling had collapsed while they were crouched
over the seismograph. Much to the irritation of the owner George was
explaining that there must be a freak condition at play, which he
would like to explore further. In fairness to him I should emphasize
that this was a rare exception to his usually reliable guidance in such
situations.

Some of my most exciting moments arose on overseas ventures.
Following the devaluation of the pound against the dollar from $4.20
to $2.80, I spent three months in Peru's copper mines, acquiring some
major contracts from US companies which had traditionally bought
from our competitors, Du Pont and Hercules. Most of the mines were
located between 13,000 and 17,000 feet and every third weekend I
came down to Lima to recharge my batteries.

On one visit I met the ICI Chairman, Lord McGowan, who was the
prime architect of the inspiring merger which created the ICI Group
from four companies. He was a godlike figure to young recruits like me,
particularly as Nobel Industries was the company he had led prior to
the merger. We briefly chatted at the British Embassy in Lima, but at
dinner he sat next to the Ambassador, while I was at the end of the top
table. During the meal I saw him write on his place card, which came
along the table, and I was astonished to find it addressed to me,
because I did not think he even knew my name. His cryptic message
said: 'Lead me to the nearest lavatory quickly.' Having no idea of the
geography of the Embassy I signalled to the nearby Commercial
Attaché and as the great man stood up we led him to the nearest loo.
He emerged looking only a little happier, uttering the immortal words,
'Bloody curry!' It left a consoling thought that even godlike figures,
who I had assumed could never make a bad judgement or decision, and
whose bodily functions must equally be beyond reproach, might come
down to earth sometimes!

Another interesting experience on this visit to Peru was flying in a Constellation. This was then the most luxurious aircraft available, but the flight nevertheless involved ten landings and crossing the Atlantic from the Azores to Bermuda. There were no night stops and we arrived in Lima fifty hours later. Though hard to believe now, it was luxury travel in those far off days.

Six months later, in contrast to the altitude of 17,000 feet in the Peruvian Andes, I was 9,000 feet underground in a South African gold mine. One purpose of this visit was to introduce a new product called Ignitercord, designed to carry a flame along a 'stope' face igniting 100 or more safety fuses protruding from the explosive charges, whereas in the past each fuse had to be lit individually by hand. Ignitercord was perceived as having real potential to improve the safety and convenience of a wide range of blasting operations, and this proved to be the case. I also introduced new advanced blasting techniques in shaft-sinking operations both in the Rand mines and in the Orange Free State, where mines were in the development phase.

Finally, I visited the copper mines in what was then Northern Rhodesia, and the scale and technology of the mining techniques were the most impressive I had seen anywhere.

In March 1952 I was on a British Airways plane *en route* to Egypt, the prime purpose being to blow up a coffer dam which had been erected adjacent to the Aswan Dam so that a hydro-electric power station could be built there. After leaving Rome, the pilot announced that serious anti-British riots were taking place in Cairo, but that he would make a brief stop there for anyone who felt they must disembark, before flying on to Nairobi.

I was one of the small band of passengers who reluctantly opted to leave the plane at Cairo and, needless to say, our luggage was examined in great detail. Unfortunately in my briefcase were some plans headed 'Demolition of Aswan Dam', the word 'coffer' having been carelessly omitted. Without ceremony I was put into a prison cell at the airport, feeling very helpless as there was no way to contact either the British Embassy, which was on fire, or my ICI colleagues. A few hours later, the Egyptian colonel who was in charge of proceedings came to question me. I convinced him that my visit was entirely friendly and that as a military man he could see the explosive charges indicated on my plans would not blow even a small hole in the main Aswan Dam. He agreed that I could go and asked where I would stay. I was booked into the Semiramis Hotel but he strongly advised against this as some British people had been shot dead in that vicinity and, in any case, there was no way I could get any transport from the airport. He generously suggested a 'safe' house near his own home where some British people stayed; when he was relieved, he would drive me there. I lay low in this haven and forty-eight hours later we got a 'green light' from the Embassy to move about, so I took the train down to Aswan, where everything was peaceful. Two weeks later we successfully blew up the Aswan coffer dam!

My adventures on this trip, however, were not at an end, as I had to visit a manganese mine on the Sinai Peninsula. It was arranged that my ICI colleagues would deliver me to a hotel in Port Tewfick to stay overnight before being picked up next morning by the mining company. I was quite pleased about this as I would be in the Canal Zone and presumably surrounded by British troops. After sitting in the hotel lounge for two hours without seeing a single soldier I asked the hotel manager when the troops came into the hotel. He replied simply, 'Never – it is out of bounds.' He then went on to say I was the first British visitor to have stayed there for six months! It is the only time in my life that I moved a chest of drawers to seal off the bedroom door.

The Arctic was my next stop in May 1952 to visit the Spitzbergen coal mines which lie within 700 miles of the North Pole. I sailed with representatives from the Norwegian government and the local explosive manufacturer in the first coal boat to penetrate the ice cap that May. In those days ships could only reach the island for four or five months in the summer and there were no flights. Our main purpose was to investigate an underground gas explosion, attributed to the use of explosives during the winter, and I was able to advise them how to avoid future occurrences.

During the Second World War the Germans invaded Spitzbergen and continued to work the coal mines, employing the Norwegian miners under great duress. The General Manager told me there were tons of German explosives still in their magazines and asked if I would test a sample to establish if they could still be used underground. I reluctantly had to agree that they could. However, when the first few cases arrived at the coal face, the miners refused to use them. The General Manager realized that he would have had a strike on his hands if he persisted, so he asked me to supervise the destruction of the whole stock. We did this with great pleasure and gusto, using some cases to blow up small icebergs which might have been hazards to smaller boats coming into the harbour.

On a business trip to America I visited a coal mine in Beckley, West Virginia, and was impressed to find the President of the mining company eager to welcome me at 7 a.m. He soon explained the reason – his name was Haslam and he had never met anyone before of this name. So I got a big order for explosives and detonators for being a Haslam! On returning to the surface he said that his wife would like me to join a small luncheon party at their home. On arrival I found no fewer than sixty guests were waiting to welcome his English namesake. Many years later Joyce and I had a weekend break in Nassau and when we registered at the hotel the receptionist said another Haslam was a fellow guest – by a remarkable coincidence my acquaintance from Beckley. As a result of this second meeting he arranged to come to England and visited Bolton, where the name Haslam is as common as Smith. My father took him around cemeteries, churches and registry offices and he left happy, convinced that he had finally established his family tree.

In 1953 I was offered a plant superintendent's job at our main Ardeer factory in Scotland, which I foolishly declined on the grounds that I would no longer be using my mining experience. In those days career planning and management development were in their infancy and this important aspect of the offer was lost on me.

I benefited greatly by attending a management course at Henley Administrative Staff College (now Henley Management College). It made me realize that I was really operating like a one-man band, while many contemporaries on the course were already being exposed to broader management roles. The penny then really dropped! In early 1955 I was made Assistant Manager of the Technical Service Department with responsibility for the Explosives Section and its commendable team of mining engineers and demonstrators.

In 1956 my manager, Robert Westwater, and I were in discussions with David Lean, the director, and Sam Spiegel, the producer, of the proposed film *Bridge on the River Kwai*. Spiegel wanted to use a model of the bridge but David Lean was determined not to go ahead without an actual bridge. The purpose of the meeting was to assure the producer that the bridge could be blown up with absolute certainty. The film was shot in Ceylon in 1957 and my colleague, David Brook, went out to supervise the blast.

Once the blast had been prepared, intricate organization was needed for the bridge to be blown at precisely the time the train passed over with its crowd of dummy Japanese soldiers. The cameras had to be placed accurately to achieve optimum value from the spectacle. Along the route of the approaching train were signal points connected to the bunker where David Brook would fire the blast. Coloured bulbs in front of him would light up as each stage was reached. A key light would show when the driver adjusted his controls to leap clear, allowing the train to rattle on towards its doom.

On the first attempt, however, the blast failed and the driverless train careered across the bridge and went straight through the emergency barrier which was intended to stop it. It landed in an upright position in the middle of a road. Getting the first news flash in Glasgow, we pondered on our earlier guarantee to Sam Spiegel! However, what had happened was that a key cameraman had not illuminated his bulb and, rightly, David Brook did not fire the blast. This unexpected hitch delayed the sequence for twenty-four hours while railway employees dragged the engine and coaches back and replaced them on the rails. Next day the operation was repeated with great success, the bridge collapsing just as the train reached the critical point, and was subsequently seen by millions of cinemagoers all over the world.

In newspaper reports many years later during my period in British Steel and British Coal, I became 'the man who blew up the Bridge on the River Kwai'! For reasons unknown to me it was repeated time after time and, much as I tried to have the error corrected in press records, I had no success. This was a continuing embarrassment to me and more importantly to David Brook, who deserved the real recognition for this spectacular achievement.

At this time Nobel Division, in collaboration with ICI (India), was building an explosives factory at Gomia in Bihar, and we were asked to receive and train a newly elected Indian chief inspector of explosives. He was due to visit our detonator factory near Polmont, travelling from Glasgow by train to the nearby station. However, he was taken ill during the night but failed to inform us. By a remarkable coincidence, another Indian was on the train and got off at Polmont Station – the chances of this happening must have been millions to one. Much to his amazement a waiting chauffeur ushered him into the waiting factory car.

'Jumbo' Cattle was a fine example of a works manager of the old school, who received distinguished visitors with considerable dignity. However, this time he rang me with much irritation to say he could not communicate with his visitor, who spoke no English. I replied this was extraordinary, as he spoke perfect English before leaving Glasgow. Fortunately there was a factory worker who had been a missionary in India and spoke some Hindi, so the visitor was able to explain that he had come to repair some fairground machinery in Falkirk. He had thought when passing through the police gate into the factory that he was being jailed, and could not understand why he was being received in such style by the governor!

About this time I became aware that ICI had compiled a list of people perceived as having high potential, and I was on it. In April 1957, James Lambert, then Managing Director of Nobel Division, summoned me to his office and announced to my surprise that I was to become the division's staff manager. Furthermore he was telling me, not asking me. The Personnel Director, Angus Richardson, was highly experienced in all aspects of management and helped me greatly in settling into this new vocation. I was also fortunate to inherit a splendid team from my predecessor, George Wilson.

This was a demanding period as the division had grown rapidly during the war, supplying military explosives and detonators to the armed forces and also managing some government ordnance factories. These activities had obviously steadily declined and growing mechanization in UK coal mines was beginning to reduce the needs of our major consumer. These factors led to major factory closures and a serious cutback at our main operation at Ardeer in Ayrshire.

Two other significant events impacted adversely on the division's affairs. Firstly, we had been supplying safety fuse for nearly all the South African gold mines. Our partner in our explosives business there, the Anglo-American Corporation, felt understandably that as safety fuse demand had grown to such a high level, the time had come to establish a factory there. The sad consequence was the closure of our Cornish factory at Tuckingmill near Camborne, which had had a long and distinguished history, having been created by the Bickford Smith family in 1831. Michael Bickford Smith, great great grandson of the founder, was the current Works Manager. I accompanied John Holm, then Divisional Managing Director, to announce the closure and will never forget the terrible shock and sadness of the employees, as they and their families had relied on jobs at the Tuckingmill factory for generations. As usual we offered everyone an appropriate job at other ICI factories in the UK, but only a handful of employees accepted. However, in the best Cornish traditions, several were willing to move with their families to South Africa!

Secondly, the Nobel Division had already developed a burgeoning speciality chemical business and, with the decline of explosives, the board was determined to expand this sector. One successful venture, for example, was to enter the silicones market.

The next major innovation was the development of a new fibre known as Ardil. The raw material was peanuts from the notorious Groundnut Scheme launched by the British government after the Second World War to help feed, with this high-protein staple crop, the rapidly growing population of East Africa – but it proved to be a costly failure. A group of high flyers within the Division were charged with developing, manufacturing and marketing this product. Everything seemed to be going well and a commercial scale plant was built at our Dumfries factory. The new fibre had a remarkably soft feel, far superior to wool or cashmere, but the project did not prosper because its physical characteristics could not stand up to the demands of intensive textile machinery. The announcement to abandon the project and the plant was the most shattering event I had ever attended. Expectations had been so high and I will never forget the shocked reactions of those involved.

I believe that any retrenchment which involves massive manpower redundancies is the most demanding management task. ICI had not had to face such a major cutback since the 1930s and it was necessary to upgrade the generosity of the company's redundancy terms in order to carry through these difficult closures with the maximum of consideration and compassion. It was a lesson which was to serve me well during the rest of my career.

Life was not without its lighter moments. One of our tasks was to arrange head-office functions and a particularly memorable occasion was a Burns Night in our Glasgow office restaurant, which had a highly polished parquet floor. It was obvious when the piper entered to pipe in the haggis that he was drunk, and half way to the top table there was a terrible wail from his bagpipes as he collapsed on the floor. The chef, who was carrying the haggis above his head, fell over the recumbent piper and the silver tray slid like a sledge across the floor, hitting a leg of the top table – but the haggis sped on like a curling stone before crashing into a wall. It had to be dusted down before being replaced on the tray and put in its rightful place on the top table, where one of my colleagues had the unenviable task of declaring the Ode. Meanwhile, the prostrate piper was carried from the scene in disgrace, followed by the distraught chef.

Another memory of the same restaurant floor concerned a waitress who slipped and broke her wrist. Soon after the incident I received a report from our Safety Officer that it was essential to spend £2,000 to rough up the floor to prevent future accidents. About this time the first ski slope had opened in Scotland and some of our young Glasgow employees formed a ski club. They asked me if the company would loan them £2,000 to launch it. The same night as I signed the document to rough up the restaurant floor, I came out of the office lift to find that the ski club had built a minor dry ski slope down the main staircase with the money we had loaned them, and were sliding down with great gusto into a blank wall. The contrast of our approach to safety at work and leisure pursuits has puzzled me ever since!

In early 1960 I became Personnel Director of Nobel Division and had my first experience of serving on a board and seeing a business in the round. I could not have had a better chairman than James Craik to help me make this transition. He was a man of small stature but with outstanding leadership qualities, blending the board into an excellent team and giving us clear objectives on how to progress the business in this demanding period in the division's history. He also had the commendable ability to challenge us with specific tasks and targets within our own sphere of influence, which kept us highly motivated. I learned a great deal about the role of a chairman from him and was able to put this into practice in my future career.

I was also asked to chair an ICI company panel to devise a scheme to assess salaried posts across the company, from the lowest-paid jobs up to middle managers. At that time schemes had become well established for evaluating weekly paid jobs for process and related workers, but our early researches showed that virtually no such scheme existed in the UK for the type of posts we were to study. The panel had a long title, but quickly became abbreviated to the Haslam Panel. I had a talented team of colleagues, who covered all major staff functions, and we spent a week every month evaluating jobs across ICI divisions. Once a month we had a weekend together at a comfortable retreat to review our findings and to develop a formula which truly reflected the content of this wide range of jobs.

It was impossible not to be impressed with the pride our staff took in even the most humble roles, and the incidents we encountered could fill a book. For example, we asked a supply clerk at our alkali division what the most difficult decision he personally had to take was and he mentioned the supply of toilet paper to major sites. He had to establish emergency stocks with local suppliers and it was his sole responsibility whether to call up these stocks if a diarrhoea outbreak hit one of their sites! The most meticulous man we met was the Services Foreman at our Grangemouth works. Asked to describe his job he took a deep breath and said he was responsible for five sites, A site, B site, C site, D site and E site. He also looked after eight railway sidings, which he listed in full: Number 1 siding, Number 2 siding, and so on. Then he said he was responsible for 150 people and started to name them all. I said we were impressed to hear he knew everyone in his team, but it was not necessary for us to know all their names!

Eighteen months later the final formula emerged during an all-night sitting at the Marine Hotel, North Berwick. The scheme was based on fifteen grades; for example, most graduates on joining were on Grade 11.

After the scheme was launched it quickly became known as the Haslam Scheme, and my name was recognized as the most familiar in ICI. When I met members of staff, rather than announce their names they would say, 'I am Haslam 9', or whatever their grade. This persisted for many years. Much to my amazement, on a visit to Taiwan some fifteen years later, by which time I was the ICI Personnel Director, a young Chinese girl came up to me and said, 'I have been Haslamized today.' She then asked me why I had been named after a verb. Such was fame!

In January 1962 I was seconded to the southern sales region as Deputy Regional Manager to gain some commercial experience, and I realized for the first time that I was being given the career development treatment. In those days ICI sold nearly all its products in the UK through regional offices, each division having its own sales manager in each office. The overall Regional Manager of Southern Region was Eric Parker, one of the most experienced and able marketing executives in ICI and, incidentally, the brother of Cecil Parker, the film star. Individual regional sales managers were all top-drawer performers. I benefited enormously from this exposure, which embraced involvement in the wide range of techniques used in selling ICI's very diverse products.

It was the intention that after this secondment I should return to Nobel Division, but much to my surprise the Board's Appointments Committee decided that I should move on to Plastics Division as Commercial Director. I was puzzled at this turn of events and some years later a document came my way indicating that John Sisson, then Plastics Division Chairman, had made a particular request for me. He explained that he had seen me in action and was impressed by my sharp commercial mind. My own recollection was that I had only met him once, playing liar dice together late one evening at ICI's education centre!

This sudden switch from explosives to plastics was to prove yet another unexpected but beneficial career move.

4
ICI Plastics Division: 1963–9

I viewed my move in January 1963 to Plastics Division as Commercial Director with some trepidation, but was extremely fortunate to have at the helm such a powerful and congenial trio as John Sisson, the Chairman, and his two deputy chairmen, Edward Williams and Douglas Owen. They took me through a quick learning curve, so I soon felt able to make a contribution.

Plastics Division was a different world – it was clearly rapidly expanding, but there were some dark clouds developing. The key PVC patents had already expired and prices had plunged; and the patents on polythene, which ICI had invented, were about to expire. As ICI had licensed the know-how widely round the world, there were several licensees poised to become vigorous global competitors.

About this time Peter Allen, soon to become ICI Chairman, was dining with us at our Welwyn headquarters and he expressed the view that the basic polythene polymer could fall from its then current level of about 4 shillings (20p) per pound to 1s. 6d (7½p). We expressed our doubts about this but he was only proved wrong by the price rapidly plunging to 1s (5p) per pound, which had a devastating effect on the division's profits.

Later in 1983 the ICI board decided to employ the management consultants McKinsey to look at the company's management structure. Plastics was one of the two divisions chosen for detailed scrutiny and I was a liaison link with the McKinsey team. Their investigation did not get off to a propitious start, as it was found that the two youngest team members had recently been interviewed for jobs at ICI and turned down! John Sisson rightly complained about this and more mature consultants were flown in from New York.

Seeing consultancy in action, it seemed to me to be an easy way of making a living. I do not remember a really original thought emerging from their efforts that was not already in the minds of our own management team. I rather grudgingly accepted that their skill was to act as a catalyst in putting together these wide-ranging ideas into a cohesive package, which in turn carried their prestigious stamp. As we all expected, McKinsey recommended that the division should be split into four groups, each a separate profit centre led by its own division director.

As a result, I was delighted to inherit the Films Group, which was in an embryonic stage of development. It embraced polythene film, already being widely used and growing rapidly; polypropylene film, which was eventually to replace cellophane in many packaging applications; and, most importantly, Melinex polyester film, destined to become the Rolls-Royce film product, used in X-ray films and many other demanding applications. Eventually Melinex became a very attractive global profit earner for ICI. It was a pleasure, too, to find that the first Melinex equipment was being erected in the building at the Dumfries factory which had housed the ill-fated Ardil plant. It was really uplifting to find some of the redundant employees getting renewed work in the same setting.

This was one of the most creative periods of my business life and I was supported by an incredibly able and enthusiastic team at a time of extraordinary expansion. We were selling almost 3,000 tons of Melinex film per annum and my two closest lieutenants, marketing and planning colleagues Austin Gibson and Arthur Burgess, persuaded me that we should double the size of our plant at Dumfries and also build our first new plant in Europe. These two expansion proposals went through the ICI board while the Division Chairman was away for over three months enjoying a sabbatical leave. On his return he sent for me and said, 'You must be out of your mind', pointing out that these two projects would increase our yearly capacity overnight from 3,000 to 12,000 tons.

I went to Switzerland on holiday and on the way back I suddenly thought: Oh my God, what have I done? I immediately went to Dumfries, where they were already digging an enormous hole for the second plant. I began to get cold feet, but my two colleagues were proved absolutely right. Those two new plants came on stream at a time when we needed all the Melinex they could produce. It was a period of risk-taking and setting horizons for growth rates which were well beyond anything I had experienced before or since.

Melinex was also my first experience of marketing a new product in the USA where, incidentally, we had to compete with Du Pont's equivalent product, Mylar. In those days Plastics Division sold its product in the US market through an agency run by Jeffrey Henriques and his son, the father being one of the best salesmen I have ever encountered. With the assistance of our UK technical service people, they built the market so quickly that our USA sales soon began to catch up with our combined sales in the UK and Europe, a development which led to us building a Melinex plant in Hopewell, Virginia. I learned two important lessons from this: first that customers in the USA were much more willing to chance their arm with a new product than their European counterparts; and secondly, because of the sheer size of many US customers, like 3M, a trial order could match a year's supply for a UK customer in the same business.

Sealing one major contract with a major US account, General Aniline (GAF), had a humorous outcome. The President and his purchasing vice president, both avid golfers, said they would only sign the contract in the Clubhouse at St Andrews. They flew into Prestwick and we played the first round at Turnberry. On one green Ash Rigby, my ICI colleague, was bunkered and asked our purchasing visitor to walk 30 yards across the green so that he would not hit him. But this was precisely what happened, leaving him with an impressive bump on the forehead. Next day we were playing the sixteenth hole at St Andrews and the same visitor fell to the fairway with a cut bleeding on the back of his head. The President said he was determined to finish his round, but fortunately an ICI colleague walking round with us took the injured man to the local hospital. My old Nobel Division friend, Angus Richardson, was a member of the House Committee at St

Andrews and had kindly arranged for us to have a private room for lunch and the contract signing. Eventually our injured visitor returned, heavily bandaged and looking pale, but he graciously signed the contract along with his president. Two weeks later, after returning to the USA, he wrote to me saying he had never known anyone go to such extreme lengths to get him to sign a sales contract. He jokingly added: 'From my arrival in Scotland I was pulverized with golf balls and signed the contract in a semiconscious state, and I declare it null and void!'

Melinex provided my first opportunity to be involved in a negotiation with the Russians, as they had asked Simon Carves to tender for a polyester film plant based on our know-how. These negotiations dragged on for a long time but eventually reached the final stage when we met one Saturday with Mr Kustandov, the Politbureau member for the chemical industry. The prime reason why the USSR wanted the polyester film was to make capacitors, which had a valuable military use, and both the UK and US governments had to give their approval to these negotiations. Kustandov opened the meeting by attacking me and my team, saying: 'We don't really need your know-how, as we can make the film ourselves, so why should we pay you a few million pounds?' He had a PA called Burtsov who was very helpful to us, as we encouraged him by supplying his favourite drink, Scotch whisky. Burtsov was asked to fetch a reel of their polyester film, but when it was rolled out on the table it was obvious, even to me, that it was a crude polythene film. The process was repeated a second time, but the next sample proved to be polypropylene film. On the third attempt the film was indeed polyester film, but had holes all over it. Rather sarcastically, I said this was an extremely interesting film but I could not imagine how they had manufactured it, nor how they could make capacitors from it. Kustandov said they could easily cut them out between the holes. I replied that on the basis of this sample we were selling our know-how far too cheaply. Not a word was spoken across the table for the next twenty minutes. At that point I and all our delegation folded up our papers and walked out. As we left one of their team said they would see us at 10 a.m. the next day. We turned up, as requested, and the contract was signed – but no Mr Kustandov!

In 1968 the Films Group made several acquisitions. Our major subsidiary, British Visquen Ltd, a joint venture with the Dickinson Robinson Group, bought Anglo American, a commercial plastics subsidiary, to add to our strong position in all aspects of our polythene film business. We also formed a new company, Sidex Ltd, a joint venture with British Sidac, to extend our penetration of the rapidly growing polypropylene film market.

Our most notable acquisition was Bexford, jointly owned by BXL Plastics and Ilford. Bexford was Europe's leading manufacturer of photographic film base. Acetate film had been the conventional base but it became clear that polyester was going to capture the market for X-rays and other demanding applications. So it was essential for Bexford to be able to produce polyester film base. Richard Probart, the Managing Director, continued in this role and the business well exceeded our expectations in sales of polyester film base. Surprisingly the acetate film business, which we anticipated would decline, also continued to expand with increased usage in industrial and packaging applications. Bexford was undoubtedly one of the best acquisitions I ever made.

Running the Films Group was one of the most pleasant and satisfying experiences of my whole career. I was in charge of a business for the first time – a business in a creative mode with considerable and rapid profit potential.

I was promoted to Deputy Chairman of Plastics Division in 1966, and this gave me exposure to a broader view of all the division's activities. Although our two major established profit earners, polythene and PVC, had entered a period of turmoil, with prices plunging rapidly, on the credit side these price levels created a massive range of new applications, particularly for polythene – for example, bags for all kinds of shop products and large sacks for fertilizers. However, it took years to adjust to this radical change. We had to restructure and sharply improve the productivity of our own operations and our petrochemicals division had to build substantially larger catalytic cracker plants to produce ethylene – the starting block – at a much lower price. Our potential customers, engaged in converting the polythene into this ever-growing range of new applications, had to install a vast amount of new equipment. Eventually, after much sustained effort over several years, polythene was restored to a mature level of profitability.

The year 1969 brought another exciting move, this time to ICI Fibres as Deputy Chairman, with the intention that I would take over as Chairman in 1971.

5
ICI Fibres: 1969–74

I joined ICI Fibres when Edward Abbot was Chairman and his predecessor, George Whitby, the ICI board director carrying the fibres portfolio. Both were founder members of the original fibres team who had made major contributions to its successful development, so I was fortunate in having such experienced tutors in smoothing my entry into what proved to be my most complex industry so far.

My immediate responsibilities as Deputy Chairman embraced commercial, sales, and marketing activities and I had a splendid team of fellow directors: Denys Marvin, destined to become a distinguished managing director of AE&CI Ltd, our joint venture with Anglo-American in South Africa, and Norman Mims and Brian Smith, who became successive chairmen of ICI Fibres after my departure.

Although ICI Fibres was having its best year ever, I quickly became aware that the storm clouds were already gathering. Du Pont had invented nylon in 1939 and ICI became their licensee in the UK. Initially ICI had decided to manufacture nylon polymer and to enter into a partnership with Courtaulds, with whom it had a friendly relationship, to manufacture and sell nylon fibres. Eventually a joint company, with ICI and Courtaulds as equal partners, was formed with the name of British Nylon Spinners (BNS) and from 1965 its operations came directly under ICI Fibres control. The basic Du Pont nylon licences expired in 1956 and a global battle for market share developed, but the market was still not saturated and profits remained high until 1965, when a steady decline began.

The story of Terylene was simpler. The product was patented in 1941 when the inventor, J.R. Winfield, was working for the Calico Printers' Association (CPA). However, it was 1947 before CPA gave ICI exclusive rights for its manufacture and sale world-wide, except the USA where the rights were sold to Du Pont with ICI's assistance. ICI had the right to sublicense third parties world-wide and decided to exercise it to the full. It licensed companies in most other major European countries, to Teijin Ltd and Toyo Rayon in Japan, and also to its own subsidiaries in Canada, South Africa, Australia and India.

By extending the life of the basic CPA patent to 1968, Terylene remained very profitable. When I joined ICI Fibres in early 1969 profits were running at an all-time high. Thereafter, as increasing supplies of both nylon and polyester fibres flooded into our markets, much of it from our own licensees, it was all downhill. In 1969, for example, nylon fibre prices fell by over 20 per cent.

After our similar experience with polythene in Plastics Division I reflected on the virtues of wide-scale licensing of unique inventions with global potential. The problem, of course, was that ICI could not visualize how to finance the development of either polythene or Terylene on a global basis. Hence the attractive alternative was to generate a lucrative flow of royalties for the next fifteen to twenty years. However, when patent protection falls away in such a situation, everyone believes they can grab 5 per cent of everybody else's market without actually losing any of their own! So everyone overexpands their capacity and these collective misjudgements create a disastrous situation. It can take many years to readjust to a new, highly competitive market, and although the product can eventually be restored to reasonable profit, it is never at the glamorous initial level. This is the predictable life cycle of such unique inventions and it is a delusion to think otherwise.

One of the conditions of our contracts with our polyester licensees was to hold annual conferences to advise them of new commercial and technical developments. These conferences were hosted by a different licensee each year and were enjoyable, as wives joined the social events. *Der Spiegel* began to take an interest in these gatherings, enquiring, 'Why are they here?' – the implication being that we were there to discuss prices! We decided that ICI, as the founder member, should host the final conference in Malta, and booked the newly opened Grand Hotel Verdala, believing this to be a discreet location away from such prying eyes. However, we did not realize that we were the first group to have a major conference at the hotel, and at the airport we were received in great style by the Mayor of Valetta and his colleagues, who invited us next day to a reception at the Town Hall!

Michael Clapham, who was then an ICI Deputy Chairman, had his boat moored in Malta. He rang to ask if I had the ICI plane with me, if so, he could fly back to London with us. When we met at the airport the mayoral party was there in force to see us off. Michael turned up later wearing shorts and a shirt, covered in oil and with a kit-bag over his shoulder. The mayoral party were somewhat bewildered when I introduced him as my senior boss. On the flight back our captain reported that strong headwinds would force us to stop at Nice. Michael immediately asked him to book a private room at the airport for us to have a glass of champagne. This we regarded as real class!

The peak year for ICI Fibres was 1969, with a £32 million profit, which I suppose in current terms would be in the region of £400 million. But this soon collapsed and by 1971 we had a loss of £14 million, which sadly coincided with my first year as Chairman. This was a shattering experience for all ICI Fibres employees, who had been riding on the crest of a wave as the outstanding profit generators in the ICI family and suddenly found themselves at the bottom of the league.

I certainly learned the subtle art of 'keeping up appearances' despite the business seeming to collapse around us. The most important need was to keep up morale by generating an air of confidence, even though I was feeling anything but that way inclined. It was essential to give a firm impression that the board was in control of affairs, had a clear strategy and was determined to restore our business to an element of its former glory. At the same time I realized that I was involved in yet another major retrenchment exercise.

Business stresses were compounded in 1971 by the realization that my mother and father could no longer support themselves in our Bolton family home, despite having marvellous neighbours, the

Hamiltons, who had looked after them so caringly for many years. We decided they should move to a nearby nursing home in Harrogate. Surprisingly, however, my mother, who had been the strong one, died suddenly from a heart attack – almost certainly due to the strain of looking after my father, who had serious medical problems for years. My father obviously decided that life without my mother was not for him and he died peacefully just two months later. They had been wonderful parents and I will never forget them or the great sacrifices they made for me.

The other complex factor for ICI Fibres was our relationship with the UK textile industry. In 1961 ICI had made a bid to take over Courtaulds and at chairmen level all seemed to be progressing well. But I understand that two young Turks on the Courtaulds board, Frank Kearton and Arthur Knight, swayed their colleagues away from grasping this opportunity.

Both companies recognized that if their future businesses were to prosper, then the UK textile industry would have to be modernized to match the standards developing rapidly in the USA and Japan. The deal having collapsed, both companies decided to invest in some of the major UK textile companies, to help revitalize the industry. Having decided it was necessary to strengthen the UK cotton textile area, ICI in 1963 took a 20 per cent holding in Viyella International, and a 12½ per cent interest in Carrington and Dewhurst and in English Sewing Cotton. In 1964 they acquired a 20 per cent holding in Listers, a worsted manufacturer. Courtaulds followed much the same policy but there was a fundamental difference of approach: the ICI concept was to support the textile industry, whereas Courtaulds were determined to control it and eventually managed their fibre and textile interests as one integrated entity. In contrast, ICI's fibre activities had an arm's length relationship with our textile involvements and never interfered in their management. In 1970 ICI arranged the merger of Viyella International and Carrington and Dewhurst and became a 64 per cent shareholder in the new operation, Carrington Viyella.

Although ICI did not have such a dominant position in the textile business as Courtaulds, its own interests were substantial. In the next decade it proved necessary to take a large financial interest in the industry to ensure that its fibre business would develop and prosper; it is difficult to see how this could have been achieved without ICI taking the sort of action it did. Nevertheless, I still believe the acquisition of Courtaulds by ICI would have been far and away the best solution for the optimum development of the UK's textile and fibres industries in the highly competitive global market which was rapidly emerging.

I got to know the leaders of the textile industry very well. They were a fairly mixed group but I enjoyed jousting with them and many became good friends. Joe Hyman of Viyella was certainly the most extraordinary chairman with whom I had to deal. However, he deserved a great deal of credit for rationalizing and modernizing the cotton industry in Lancashire. He had an extremely sharp financial brain and an almost hypnotic negotiating style. I decided it was inadvisable to take any final decision in his presence, but to withdraw and reflect before finally responding.

At the same time he was extremely unpredictable. For example, we were supplying Viyella with 30,000 pounds of polyester staple fibre weekly. He rang and asked what the price would be if they began ordering 300,000 pounds weekly? We explained that unless he had recently acquired a vast number of mills of which we were not aware, this seemed rather academic. He angrily said, 'You can't tell us what to do and we'll send a weekly order for this quantity', so we supplied them at this excessive level for about ten weeks. By then nearly all the warehouse space in all the Lancashire mills was full of polyester staple fibre and his management team were screaming for us to stop.

By a stroke of good fortune, at that time he began negotiating to acquire Cyril Lord's Northern Ireland carpet business, which was in trouble. He rang me to say he needed £2million to clinch the deal and estimated that all this polyester staple fibre we had been sending him was worth about this amount. If we were to remunerate him for this vast stock he would also guarantee that we would get their nylon carpet business, which was currently being supplied from Holland. We agreed but declined to move the stock of polyester staple, which they could now pay for as they required it.

Another, more dramatic, incident occurred one Friday evening when we had been negotiating in a suite on top of the Royal Garden Hotel. Our teams filtered away to catch the last trains to the north and we two were left on our own. Joe Hyman normally did not drink alcohol, at least in public, but that night we drank a few whiskies together. About midnight he stood up and said dramatically: 'I think I will commit suicide now', and began walking towards the balcony. I am absolutely sure he would not have done so, but I grabbed and held him. We then went down in the lift together to his Rolls-Royce, which was waiting outside, and he said: 'You have saved my life tonight so you get in the car and it will take you to your flat.' I said there was no reason why we shouldn't both get in the car but he repeatedly declined and eventually I drove off, leaving him standing on the apron in front of the hotel. On the following Monday morning, when Joyce and I were driving down to Dover to have a brief holiday in France, I was reading *The Times*. In a business page report Joe expressed his dismay at ICI Fibres' lack of understanding about the needs of his company and said that our recent negotiations had demonstrated this to the full. He had presumably held a press conference at his home on Sunday, but on Monday morning he had driven all the way up to Harrogate to apologize personally to me. He was met by Denys Marvin, who explained that I was in Le Touquet, but insisted he would wait until I came back and settled down rather uneasily in our Crimple Guest House, before finally moving on two days later!

A more profound problem arose just before Christmas 1971. Joe usually held an annual reception in the ballroom at Claridges and always had an impressive guest list. This year was no exception as Harold Wilson, then Prime Minister, and many of his Cabinet colleagues and their wives were there. Joyce and I had not spoken to Joe all evening, but as we left we were able to pass on our season's greetings. I also thanked him for arranging for us to be entertained for dinner by John Blackburn, his senior colleague, understandably recognizing that we were not among the prime guests, whom Joe would be hosting. When we arrived at the Savoy Grill, I quickly realized that most of the executive directors of Viyella and their wives were there. The only outsiders, besides ourselves, were Louis Goodman of Marks & Spencer and his wife.

I soon realized, too, that John Blackburn had arranged the party himself, unbeknown to Joe. I quickly sensed a feeling of mutiny around the table. At the end of the meal John took me aside and told me that at the board meeting next day they proposed to remove Joe from the chairmanship. I suddenly realized that I might well be perceived as a conspirator to this action. Next morning Joe rang his colleagues to say he had been delayed and that he would be an hour late arriving for the board meeting. He was, however, asked to stay at his flat in Grosvenor House and told that they would come to see him there. John Blackburn and Hubert Clegg, the senior non-executive director, led the delegation and gave him the message that they wished to terminate his chairmanship. Soon after they had departed Joe rang me and asked me to come to his aid. I reminded him that I was not his shareholder; that was ICI head office. He then rang Peter Allen, Chairman of ICI, but in the end it was decided we should not interfere. It really was a sad ending, as Joe Hyman had used his very considerable talents in rationalizing and modernizing some major UK textile activities but this success had been marred by flashes of eccentric behaviour.

Soon after leaving Viyella he re-emerged as the Chairman of Crowthers, the Yorkshire woollen company. When he had settled in he rang me and flatteringly said: 'Bob, I'm sure you and I can do for the Yorkshire woollen industry what we did for the cotton industry in Lancashire.' I was touched that he thought of ICI Fibres in these terms, but hastened to add that regretfully we could not afford it.

In 1958, after discussions with many potential US partners, ICI had decided to choose the Celanese Corporation of America as a partner. From the Celanese viewpoint, ICI had well-proven know-how and considerable resources. From ICI's viewpoint, Celanese was an expansionist partner with renowned commercial skills. A 50–50 company, Fibre Industries Inc (FII), was formed and proved highly successful in competing with Du Pont, combining ICI's technology and Celanese's marketing skills. The trade name of the product was Fortrel. Celanese paid ICI royalties which amounted to £12 million.

I became a board member when the company reached a mature state. The board comprised equal numbers of top ICI and Celanese representatives and was one of the most effective and exciting partnerships in which I have ever served. I also learned a great deal about marketing products in the USA from our Celanese colleagues.

In 1971 we had to determine the best way to embrace the growing use of bulked or texturized yarns. Initially this operation had been carried out by independent texturers. We decided to create the Crimplene Club – an association of texturers which bought their polyester yarns exclusively from ICI and sold the textured yarn under the Crimplene label. Moreover, our research activities indicated that texturing could be carried out very effectively as an extension of fibre manufacture and was really more akin to fibre producing than the classic textile processes.

We decided to acquire two Carrington Viyella subsidiaries, William Tatton and Aycliffe Textiles, in which ICI already had a 64 per cent involvement. The other substantial purchase was Qualitex from the Likierman family, in which ICI had a 10 per cent interest – a prominent nylon texturer but with growing polyester interests. We formed these companies into a new company, Intex Yarns, which represented 35 per cent of the total UK production of polyester and nylon textured yarns. Michael Likierman, former managing director of Qualitex, became Joint Managing Director of Intex Yarns but his tenure was short-lived, as the performance of the Qualitex factories we had acquired fell well short of our expectations.

The next step was to integrate the Intex sales into ICI Fibre's marketing activities. This new business structure fulfilled the desired objective of achieving a more rapid response to market needs, using the wider resources of ICI Fibres and Intex. The remaining independent texturers did not seem to regard this development with apprehension but welcomed it, as it clearly produced a more orderly market.

Yet another serious problem arose in 1972. The future of polyester yarns in the USA had been under similarly heavy pressure. The Nixon administration increasingly protected the market by raising tariffs, but in April suddenly more or less pulled up the drawbridge to polyester imports. Many Japanese ships were *en route* to the USA laden with polyester fibre when this happened and they turned round and headed for Europe. There was no reason why this abnormal source of imports should not have been shared across Europe, but the bulk of it came into the UK.

One large ship went into Cherbourg but the French customs explained that they would have to send a few samples to their laboratories to test for acceptable quality; if the ship waited in the port they hoped to have an answer in the next week or two! Needless to say the ship sailed immediately to Southampton where the UK officials seemed to welcome it with open arms, apparently with the desire to create even more competition in an already overloaded market. We estimated finally that about 90 per cent of these exceptional Japanese imports landed in the UK. Only trivial amounts found a home in France, Germany, Italy or Spain. There was obviously a very different approach in the USA and the other European countries to this sudden dire situation to that of the UK government.

The failure of Britain's negotiations to join the European Common Market in 1963 had led the BNS board to establish a factory at Oestringen in Germany. In the late 1960s textured polyester yarns were beginning to have a real impact in the European markets and Terylene manufacture was installed at Oestringen to meet this demand. This factory played an important role in the development of our overall European fibre activities.

On one visit to Oestringen I asked Peter Beazley, who effectively masterminded our continental fibre activities, whether I could attend a meeting of the Supervisory Board, which included four worker directors. During discussions, management indicated that they intended to increase the labour force by 300–400 employees to meet the perceived increase in demand. Much to my amazement the worker directors opposed this, as they did not believe the demand would be there, but if it should emerge, then they would work more overtime.

I was so impressed with their contribution to the meeting that on returning to Harrogate I asked Peter Standring, our Personnel Director, to arrange for some leading shop stewards from our UK factories to visit Oestringen and spend a few days with their opposite numbers there. We arranged for interpreters to be available so that they could also spend some leisure time together. When they returned we asked the delegates to come to Harrogate to hear their reactions.

The meeting started well – they had much enjoyed and appreciated the visit – but what followed was totally negative. They said: 'The German employees don't know how to behave like real trade unionists and your management there aren't challenged in the way we feel they should be. Further, if you let us return annually we think we could teach them how to behave!' Regrettably they had learned nothing, nor did they seem to register that their German colleagues and families obviously enjoyed a much better lifestyle than they did, reflecting the higher wages from much higher productivity being achieved at Oestringen. UK trade union leaders have always claimed that our productivity lags behind other European countries or the USA because companies there have been prepared to invest more capital in their production processes. However, in this case the investment and the production equipment in Germany was precisely the same as in the UK.

These years fortunately had lighter moments. Joyce and I were exposed to the more exotic world of fashion shows in the UK and Europe. A splendid one was in the auditorium of the Technical University of Helsinki, with over 1,000 guests. A show in Ireland was the most memorable, held at the famous Royal Dublin Society in the spectacular setting of the renowned Sale Ring. It did not get off to an auspicious start, as the commentator opened his remarks by saying: 'We have some splendid fillies on display tonight.' This did not go down at all well with the models, who had to be pacified before the event could start. Nevertheless, the whole evening went with a real bang. After the show the designers organized a large party where Joyce mentioned to one how much she admired a particular Crimplene dress. After midnight, with the party still in full swing, a young lady arrived, having been summoned from her bed by her boss. Joyce was asked to stand on a small dais to be measured, embarrassingly surrounded by about 300 happily inebriated onlookers. The dress soon arrived at our home, was a perfect fit and greatly admired.

In 1968 a consortium of ICI, Courtaulds, John Brown and Dobson & Barlow was building the first polyester fibres plant in the USSR at Mogilev, some 120 miles south-west of Moscow. This was based on ICI Fibres technology and fifty ICI families lived there in a five-storey block of modern flats, cheek by jowl with the Russians, most of whom also worked at the plant. A novel feature was that ICI Fibres had shipped out the equipment to build a replica of an English pub, which was named the Polyspinners Bar and became the focal social centre. We were extremely fortunate to have Bill and Joy Liddell leading our team as they really did a marvellous team job in unusual and demanding roles.

As the project was in its final stages, Joyce and I decided that we must visit it to express our sincere appreciation to the Fibres' team and their families, so in August 1972 we travelled to Moscow. On leaving the tourist areas, we had to become 'foreign specialists', travelling by train to Minsk on a Friday night accompanied by a KGB man, Victor, to keep his eye on us. He could hardly do this because we were in a de luxe sleeper and Victor was some carriages away in the bottom class! We then travelled on together by car to Mogilev on Saturday morning. From our flat in the Fibres building, we naturally looked down from the balcony. Joyce said our families seemed to be very productive, as there appeared to be more English than Russian children playing in the square below. It emerged that the Russian wives helped domestically with the Fibres families, and when our wives returned home from the UK after a break, they brought Marks & Spencer clothing for the Russian children.

Bill Liddell took me on a tour of the factory, having explained that George Harrison, a member of the Fibres team, was to marry Elena, a Russian girl, that afternoon and Joyce was invited to join all the other ICI wives at the Mogilev Palace of Weddings. George had arranged a de luxe wedding, which included having a three-piece band who said they knew some Western tunes. However, as the couple moved up to be married, they struck up 'When the Saints Go Marching In' – much to the amusement of our wives. After the ceremony they were allowed to dance a few steps together and this time the band played 'Strangers in the Night' to a waltz tempo! The whole wedding party toured the town in their cars so that the bride could place bunches of flowers at the feet of the statues of Lenin and other renowned figures. In the evening George and his bride joined us for our own celebration in the Polyspinners Bar.

My visit to the factory was most impressive. The plant was already twice as large as any Fibres plant in the UK, and was the largest single polyester plant to be built in one stage anywhere in the world. It was obvious from my discussions with Mr Zernov, the Chief Engineer and Site Director, that the Russians were highly delighted with the plant and full of praise for our people's efforts.

The ICI Fibres Board decided it would be appropriate to have a reunion for all the team and their wives who had served at Mogilev. This was held in December, when we also celebrated Bill Liddell's well-deserved OBE. So once again I was able to thank all the team for their splendid efforts, which had greatly enhanced ICI's prestige with the Russians. I added that on my return to Moscow I had met Sir John Killick, the British Ambassador, who had also visited Mogilev and was very impressed with the factory and what our team had achieved. Further, he believed it would add lustre to Britain's industrial image among the Russian business community.

In May 1973, I was invited by Golda Meir to join her at the Prime Minister's conference to celebrate Israel's twenty-fifth anniversary. It was a magnificent occasion, and on a personal level I was heartened by how many of the Israeli industrialists I met were aware of ICI Fibres and were buying our products. Michael Sieff, Deputy Chairman of Marks & Spencer, was a companion in the British party. I had held many discussions with him at their Baker Street, London, headquarters and, although we did not sell any fibre products directly to Marks, they were influential in determining what large sections of the textile industry would produce, hopefully based on our products. It was a fine opportunity to get to know him in a more informal ambience because, as I will explain in a later chapter, he became an important man in my life.

Returning to the main theme of our recovery from the disastrous result of 1971, the first year of my chairmanship, it took two years to find ourselves much better placed to face the future. A continuing retrenchment programme reduced the number of employees in fibres across the UK and Europe from 27,000 to 18,000, leading to impressive productivity achievements and a yearly saving of over £15 million. Working with our ICI Europa colleagues, we brought a unified approach to tackling the extended Common Market and the speed and breadth of our penetration into these countries in 1973 was particularly gratifying. As a result of these actions our profits in 1973 showed a swing of £35 million from the low negative results in 1971 and 1972, and we felt we were well on the way back.

On 21 February 1974, Joyce and I were invited to the Viennese Opera Ball by Franz and Träute Wilhelm, important Austrian customers. This was to be a memorable day in our lives because, as we arrived at our hotel, I had a telephone call from Jack Callard, then Chairman of ICI, informing me that I had that day been appointed to the ICI board. Our hosts' reaction was a little subdued, as they thought I was being demoted from chairman to a director, but I hastened to explain that ICI was a much larger business than ICI Fibres.

Attending the Opera Ball is physically demanding and many of the Viennese prepare by spending a week at a health farm, but we had just come from a hectic spell in Zurich. Even so, we went through the evening feeling a wonderful glow and were superbly entertained by our hosts. We finally said our farewells about 3 a.m., reluctantly accepting that we were not going to make the traditional breakfast at Sachers. We were picked up by our Austrian manager at 9 a.m. for the drive to the airport and he was still wearing his white tie and tails. We then enjoyed a celebratory bottle of champagne for breakfast!

Bob Haslam, the 17-year-old captain of Bolton School in 1940. It was wartime and, with teachers in the services, he and other seniors were called on to restore order in the form rooms and playground – without too much difficulty because of general respect for the authority of monitors

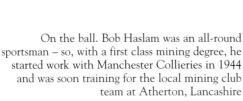

On the ball. Bob Haslam was an all-round sportsman – so, with a first class mining degree, he started work with Manchester Collieries in 1944 and was soon training for the local mining club team at Atherton, Lancashire

Working, studying and courting – Bob always recalled an epic week in June 1947 when he married Joyce Quin at St Paul's Church, Bolton, and also got his Colliery Manager's Certificate

Proud parents Bob and Joyce Haslam in 1952 with new baby son Nigel and 4-year-old Roger

Disenchanted with his coal industry prospects, Bob Haslam joined ICI's Nobel Division in 1947 specializing in explosives – seen here back at the Glasgow office, after spending most of his time on mining and demolition sites around the world

Following a succession of promotions, Bob Haslam joined the ICI board in 1974 at the age of 51, with responsibilities including ICI (India). The company presented an old dyestuffs building in Calcutta to Mother Teresa who converted it into her major home. Joyce Haslam found it a very moving, but harrowing, experience seeing wards for the dying and babies brought in from the streets

Bob and Joyce Haslam relaxing by the Thames in 1975

Bob Haslam in 1982 collected ICI's award for thirty-five years service from board colleague, John Harvey-Jones

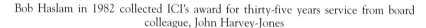

Bob Haslam at the microphone in 1984 as Tate & Lyle chairman – a post he held for four years of increasing profits

The following year he welcomed to the group's London headquarters the Archbishop of Canterbury, Robert Runcie, whose father had been electrical engineer of the Liverpool refinery. Smiling as he left, the Archbishop told his host: 'If my father, as I expect, is now looking down on this scene, he will be much prouder that I am lunching with the Tate & Lyle board, than he ever was when I became Archbishop of Canterbury!'

Knighted in 1985 on moving as chairman, from British Steel to British Coal, Sir Robert at Buckingham Palace with Lady Joyce Haslam and sons Nigel (*left*) and Roger. When the Queen delivered two sharp blows on the shoulders with the investiture sword, the new knight instinctively raised his hands to his ears. 'No need to worry – they are still there,' the Queen responded with a smile

After the ceremony granting him the freedom of the City of London in 1985, a parting presentation commemorating the event is made by the Chamberlain of London, Bernard Hasty

The British Coal chairman
becomes a companion of the
Institution of Mining Electrical
and Mining Mechanical
Engineers in 1988

Sir Robert Haslam with Prime Minister Margaret Thatcher in Downing Street,
February 1990. He always welcomed their robust and challenging exchanges

It was the pinnacle of his career when, after an interval of thirty-eight years, Sir
Robert Haslam returned to coal mining as British Coal chairman in 1986. Visiting
collieries in all coalfields, he quickly got to know the modern mining industry

In a series of pit visits, the new British Coal chairman saw for himself how machine mining had replaced the pick and shovel work of his earlier years

Profitable coal output from opencast mining operations increased by 3 million tonnes a year during his five years as chairman

British Coal chairman Sir Robert Haslam invites the Duke of Edinburgh to launch officially the new Selby mining complex in Yorkshire in 1989. 'The underground visit went extremely well, the Duke seemed to enjoy thoroughly his rapport with the miners and they responded warmly

Five years as British Coal chairman ended in 1990 with a bottom line profit of £78 million – the first for many years. Sir Robert Haslam with operations director, John Northard (*left*) and deputy chairman, Sir Kenneth Couzens

6
ICI Board: 1974–83

My nine years on the board of ICI – then Britain's leading industrial company – were in four distinct phases.

Phase 1. 1974–9
Walking through the portals of the Millbank headquarters in London on 1 April 1974 was probably the most significant event of my whole career. I had a real surge of pride at joining the ICI board and realized I was now walking the same corridors as the early greats of ICI, the Mond Family and Harry McGowan, who had been responsible for the creation of the company and for giving it such a splendid birth. I inherited one of the prime offices, with stunning views of the River Thames, and hoped this would bring inspiration. As I looked out I reflected on my boyhood days in Bolton and the many highlights of my career.

Jack Callard was my first chairman on joining the ICI board and I shall always be grateful to him for the way he smoothed my way during my settling-in period. He was a gentleman in every possible way. Nevertheless, I found the transition to being a main board director somewhat difficult. Having run the ICI Fibres business and its involvements in global activities it came as a culture shock to find myself with only a secretary and chauffeur to command!

I became the board Product Director for both Paints and Fibres, and also the Territorial Director for India and Pakistan, but these were more akin to 'ambassadorial' roles, as the individual chairmen were each charged with running their own businesses. Moreover, the UK Division and the overseas companies were monitored and controlled by the ICI board through formal control groups, each chaired by a deputy chairman, along with the appropriate product or territorial director and two or three other directors. Even as a 'new boy' I felt this was an over-elaborate way of running the company.

My Paints involvement took me back to my childhood, when I used to mix paint for my father, sitting on the floor of his decorator's shop. This was in stark contrast to ICI's already massive involvement in the global paints market, which already embraced more countries than any other ICI product. It was also a period when the Dulux brand was making striking progress. For most of the time Denys Henderson was Chairman of the division and having both worked together in Nobel Division, we slipped easily into a close relationship. Of course, Denys eventually became a successful ICI Chairman. Altogether I found my Paints involvement a rewarding one and it certainly extended my knowledge and experience of marketing.

At ICI Fibres I had been succeeded as Chairman by Norman Mims and he in turn was succeeded by Brian Smith, who eventually was to follow me in various steps of my ICI board career. Fibres in the UK and Europe was obviously a familiar scene to me and it was gratifying that the recovery of the business continued to progress under its new leaders.

The most fascinating aspect of my portfolio was my involvement in the Indian subcontinent. ICI (India) was the major element and embraced a wide range of products: fibres at Thana, agricultural products at Kanpur, paints at Hyderabad, general chemicals at Rishra, explosives at Gomia in Bihar. Plans to establish a pharmaceutical plant near Madras were also developing.

Another welcome feature was that Duggie Owen, who had been my immediate boss at Plastics Division, was now Chairman of ICI (India). Joyce and I were to have many enjoyable stays with Duggie and his wife, Pam, in the chairman's residence in Delhi, where the ICI (India) board was then based, as the perceived need was that the directors should be close to those ministers and their colleagues who were responsible for shaping India's future industrial strategy. This objective was clearly achieved.

At that time ICI (India) was probably the most profitable business in the whole ICI family, but the problem was that Indian withholding taxes were so high, that the share of profits we could repatriate to the UK was much reduced. Hence, we were constantly seeking more profitable outlets for the funds retained in India.

I visited our explosives operation at Gomia more frequently than any other factory. Having been involved in this project since its inception during my time in Nobel Division, I had a special interest in its development. Whenever Joyce and I visited the factory they usually arranged a Burns supper. By this time all the Scottish families involved in building the factory had returned home, but they had taught their Indian successors all about Burns and his works. Harrods haggises were stored in a deep freeze and could be produced whatever the time of year. They also taught some of their management successors how to play the bagpipes and with some of the main players in kilts, the ceremony continued in its classic form. Joyce and I could hardly contain ourselves when one of the managers delivered the 'Ode to the Haggis' with a pronounced Indian lilt!

Gomia became an outstanding success and reflected great credit not only on the Nobel Division people who masterminded and started up the project, but also on the Indian managers and employees who took over running the factory in commendable style. An explosives factory has an added safety dimension and I was impressed how quickly our labour force fully respected this. I also learned how to adopt a more flexible approach to productivity. On one visit to Ardeer, our major explosives factory in the UK, I saw a hole being dug among the sand dunes for the location of a new mixer for nitroglycerine explosives. The following week I was at Gomia and saw a similar hole being dug for an identical mixer. At Ardeer there were two men working in the excavation, a digger operator and a dumper driver. At Gomia there were at least 200 men, women and children digging in the sand dunes with picks and shovels and transporting the sand in baskets on their heads. Much to my surprise, management proved that the actual costs were not too different, and of course the creation of 200 rather than two jobs was a strong humanitarian plus!

Our fibres operation at Thana was operating successfully but on a modest scale. Its main product was polyester staple fibre which was blended with cotton to make shirt fabric and other comparable end uses. Unfortunately the Indian government applied a prohibitive tax on polyester to protect their cotton industry. We argued long and hard that this was counter-productive, as there was already a shortage of land on which to grow food and this could be gradually overcome if more polyester fibre 50/50 blends with cotton were made available. However, our pleas went unheeded.

Our fertilizer operation at Panki, Kanpur, was a modern factory based on the design of our latest UK unit at Billingham. The only omission was that the Indian authorities declined to have a mechanized bagging unit at the end of the process, insisting this should be manually operated to create the optimum number of jobs. Most of the men employed in this bagging operation were Untouchables and I always made a point of shaking hands with them, much to their obvious surprise and pleasure.

Visiting our Indian factories I was impressed by the commitment of the workers to the well-being of their operation. Their loyalty was beyond reproach and I cannot remember any serious stoppage due to militant action by our workers. Manning levels were higher than in our UK factories, but the wages we were paying were a fraction of those in the UK, so it was difficult to contemplate capital investments which were obviously justified in the UK.

Following our first visit to India I was anxious that Joyce and I should also visit Pakistan. At that time the only way to cross the border was at Wagah on Tuesdays. We flew to Amritsar, were driven to the border by our agents in a near-presidential type of cortège with flags flying and whistles blowing and were taken into the VIP guest house on the Indian side. Jamie Rahim, Chairman of our Pakistan company, was invited to join us. He came across the border with great reluctance as he might have been held there, particularly as he did not have his passport with him, but all was well and we passed into Pakistan.

Our two main businesses in Pakistan were paints at Lohore and Salt at Kewhra and we visited both. Jamie Rahim was an outstanding leader of our company, ably supported by his charming wife, Iran, with whom we remain close friends. We met all the other directors and senior managers at our head office in Karachi and I was immediately impressed by the calibre and ability of our team, as I had been with their colleagues in India.

Subsequent visits to Pakistan were focused on expanding the success of our existing businesses. The establishment of a polyester fibre plant emerged as the preferred candidate, accompanied by the manufacture of one of its raw materials. Eventually the ICI board endorsed these plans, which came to fruition after my time.

In September 1975 Rowland Wright succeeded Jack Callard as Chairman, after receiving an overwhelming vote in his favour from his colleagues, and he was to fulfil all our expectations as our leader. He was aware of my desire for a more 'hands-on' job and I was delighted when he offered me the role of Personnel Director, which obviously had a higher executive context and it meant, too, that I would have some troops of my own once again. This new involvement is dealt with in the next section. Meanwhile, I also retained my Paints involvement and responsibility for India and Pakistan.

In 1975 Duggie Owen and I visited Madras to view the proposed site at Ennore, about 20 miles north of the city, for our proposed pharmaceutical factory. When we arrived all the children from the adjacent fishing village rushed out to follow us and each time we changed direction they surged behind us like a tidal wave. We agreed with our pharmaceutical colleagues that the site was suitable and as the first step we built a community hall for the fishermen's families, equipped with TV and other facilities. From the outset we had a most supportive relationship.

In February 1976 Duggie Owen retired as Chairman of ICI (India) after five years' service, during which the organization prospered under his commendable leadership. He was succeeded by Krishna Mudalier, who was only the second Indian national to occupy this post. This was consistent with the ICI board's policy that key roles should no longer be filled with expatriates. Krishna persuaded us to move our head office from Delhi to Calcutta, which was clearly the business centre of India, while still maintaining a Delhi office to continue to foster our relations with government officials.

One interesting consequence was that ICI (India) presented an old dyestuffs establishment in Calcutta to Mother Teresa, who converted it into her major home there. She named it *Prem Dam* – 'gift of love'. Krishna and his wife Vanitha had a very supportive relationship with her. Whenever Joyce visited Calcutta with me, she was invited to meet Mother Teresa and to tour the home, which she found most moving but also very harrowing, seeing wards for the dying and for young children and babies brought in from the streets.

During my stewardship in India I visited the territory three times a year and often presented long-service awards to our deserving employees at functions which had a special emotive quality and were frequently family affairs. Three of these occasions were memorable; the first, in Madras, was particularly moving. When the name of one recipient was announced he emerged from his seat about 50 yards from the dais and crawled along the floor towards me. So I rushed down to meet him, presented his award and helped to carry him back to his seat. He had been hospitalized after a stroke ten days earlier but, despite the protestations of the medical staff, was determined to come and receive his award. One of the most embarrassing long-service award ceremonies of my whole career was at Thana. As usual I was sitting on a dais and heavily garlanded, but halfway through the ceremony I had a violent bilious attack and had to rush to the nearest loo. People asked why this 'godlike' figure had run off? Had someone tried to shoot him? On returning ten minutes later I received a standing ovation – which demonstrably I did not deserve! Gomia was the site of my third exceptional long-service award ceremony. To my amazement, I was asked to present fifty-eight bicycles. To do this traditionally would have been a Herculean task, but we decided the bicycles would be numbered and lined up along one side of the room and I would present each recipient with a numbered card. This worked well but our troubles were far from over because, as we returned in our car to the club, it became patently obvious that some of the recipients had never ridden a bicycle before! Moreover, as they had their families at the ceremony, they were also trying to ride with their wives on the crossbars. Altogether it was a hazardous short journey as they criss-crossed the road in front of us, frequently falling off.

In February 1977 Rowland Wright, accompanied by his wife Kath, came to India to lay the foundation stone at the Ennore site for the new pharmaceutical and agrochemicals factory. This was a remarkable and joyful occasion, attended by all the fishermen and their families from the village. At the end of the ceremony they presented Kath Wright and Joyce with large glass cases of evil-looking deep-sea fish which they had caught over the years – touchingly their prize possessions. This factory I am sure has been a real contributor to improving health standards in India.

We spent the following weekend with the Wrights and the Mudaliers at Fisherman's Cove, near Mahablipuram. It was a delightful break, enhanced by having among the guests Mrs Gandhi's elder son Rajiv and his wife Sonia. It had been anticipated that his younger brother Sanjay would succeed his mother, but in 1980 he was killed piloting his own plane. Sanjay's death led to the political rise of Rajiv and when his mother was cruelly assassinated in 1984, he became the new prime minister. We had two pleasant evenings chatting and philosophizing with them. They seemed happy with their current lifestyles and clearly had no anticipation of the future which lay before them.

After the weekend we did a brief tour of our screening station at Bangalore, our paints factory at Hyderabad and finally the fibres factory at Thana. Everywhere the Wrights visited they were greatly welcomed.

There was a rather sad footnote to the laying of the foundation stone at Ennore in that, soon after, it was washed away by a tidal wave. My reaction was: 'My God, have we got the wrong site?' However, as far as I am aware this problem has not been repeated and the project has flourished.

In 1975 Margaret Thatcher became Leader of the Conservative Opposition and when she had settled in, she came across Smith Square to our guesthouse from time to time, primarily to hear our views on the industrial scene. She normally arrived, declined a pre-lunch drink, pulled out her notebook, sat down for lunch and began to write down our words of wisdom. Once she had a twinkle in her eye when she asked the first question: 'Did you know that I was interviewed for a job by ICI at Billingham in 1947 and turned down?' There was a stunned silence around the table, as this was news to all of us, but she went on and described precisely the man who had interviewed her thirty years earlier. One of my colleagues said, 'You were obviously interviewed by Max Blench.' She went on: 'That man did not realize one of my abilities is to read writing upside down. He wrote on my form, "This young woman is very strong willed. She will be a troublemaker. ICI should not employ her." ' There was an even longer silence. I realized I was the only ICI director present who did not come from that stable and, much to my colleagues' annoyance, I broke the silence by saying: 'Sadly Mrs Thatcher you were interviewed in the wrong part of ICI.'

In March 1978 Rowland Wright retired and Maurice Hodgson took over as Chairman. This was the most unusual chairmanship contest in ICI's history. Maurice had failing eyesight for a number of years, and had one eye operated on. It was not successful and he lost his sight completely in that eye. His second eye was showing the same symptoms, and there seemed to be no prospect he could become chairman. Courageously, however, he decided to have an operation on his second eye, which restored his eyesight so that he could be a contender for the chairmanship. He and Ray Pennock were the two contenders and Maurice won the majority of his colleagues' votes. We all, nevertheless, felt a real pang for Ray as it had been felt for some time that he would become the next chairman because of Maurice's failing eyesight. Maurice proved to be a fine chairman and overcame his eyesight problem almost as though it did not exist. In this respect he was ably assisted by his remarkable secretary, Joan Macnamara.

Following the change of chairmanship I retained my roles as Personnel and Paints Product Director, but my India/Pakistan portfolio went to Philip Harvey. I found it quite a wrench to lose this role, as it had been one of my most fascinating involvements. However, in

November 1978 further changes were announced and I became Territorial Director for Sub-Saharan Africa, along with my existing Personnel Director role, handing over as Paints Director to Allan Clements. At the time Denys Henderson, the Paints Division Chairman, said: 'Bob Haslam has been a very good friend to this division and to the ICI paint interests across the world. His contribution to our improved performance over the last two years has been considerable and my colleagues and I are happy to pay tribute to the wise counsel he has given us over the last five years.'

Involvement in my new African territory was short-lived, but it had one intriguing aspect. We and the Anglo-American Corporation were joint owners of African Explosives and Chemicals Industries (AE&CI). I was ICI's senior director on the board, which involved meetings every three months in Johannesburg. Harry Oppenheimer, our chairman, was without doubt the most influential and admired industrialist in South Africa and a renowned figure on the world scene, respected for his courageous views on apartheid. Also on the AE&CI board was Julian Ogilvie Thompson, the current Chairman of Anglo-American. Particularly pleasing for me was having Denys Marvin, my former close colleague at ICI Fibres, as Managing Director of AE&CI, who was clearly doing a splendid job in this new setting. Discussions at the board were hard-hitting, with a minimum of philosophizing, and heavily focused on making profits. It was a refreshing exposure.

One humorous incident at that time occurred at the ICI Annual General Meeting, attended by the Reverend Haslam and his followers, who had already created mayhem at other major companies' AGMs by urging them to withdraw from operations in South Africa while the apartheid policy was in force. When Rev. Haslam announced his name my board colleagues began to titter, and when he asked his basic question the Chairman said: 'I will now ask Mr Haslam to reply to the Rev. Haslam.' This caused shareholders to laugh en masse, and the Reverend never recovered his composure. Unusually, Harry Oppenheimer was present at this AGM, and when I was sitting next to him at lunch, he said in his quiet way: 'I hope that young man is not a relative of yours.' To which I responded, 'Harry, how could you think of such a thing.' I have nevertheless had lingering doubts, as my grandfather was brought up in a large family and one of his brothers emigrated to South Africa, where he became a spiritualist.

Phase 2. 1975–9

I took over my role as ICI's Personnel Director with keen anticipation. A little history might be appropriate at this stage, however. Remarkably ICI had four parents – Brunner Mond, Nobel Industries, United Alkali and British Dyestuffs – and two 'midwives' – Sir Alfred Mond and Sir Harry McGowan. Mond had gone to America, apparently to consummate a deal with a company there, but McGowan arrived in the nick of time, having sailed from South Africa via Southampton with this alternative plan for an all-British merger, which was conceived on 25 September 1926 in a New York hotel. They travelled back on the *Aquitania*, writing the basis of ICI's constitution crossing the Atlantic, and the merger was announced on 7 December. It is difficult to see how such a merger of four substantial companies could be repeated in the present era.

ICI's personnel policies sprang from this early history. Some seventy-five years earlier, Brunner Mond had succeeded in combining the needs of the business to make a profit with the needs of the individuals who worked for it. This approach can be traced back to Ludwig Mond, co-founder of the company in 1870. He was a remarkable man, not only a brilliant scientist but a leader of men – far ahead of his time in providing social benefits for his employees. He often joined the night-shift teams to discuss problems of the plant and the business. Brunner Mond was among the first employers in the UK to introduce holidays with pay, ensuring employees not only had time off but could afford to go away with their families.

The development of Ludwig's policies in ICI was the work of Alfred Mond, who became the first chairman. Probably the most important strand which emerged from Brunner Mond in those early days was the acceptance of formalized systems of consultation within the new company. The ICI works council scheme came into being in 1929. McGowan addressed all the works managers and made it clear that they were to hold meetings every month with representatives of their payroll employees, to consult them in a genuine and open way about the problems of their works and their business and to listen to the views and problems of the shop-floor representatives. Subsequently, parallel meetings were held with representatives of the white-collar staff. When the divisional structure was established, another tier was added at this level as division councils and division staff committees. The final stage involved annual meetings with members of the ICI board, both for the weekly and monthly staff.

About the time I became Personnel Director a national debate was in progress on the broader issue of 'industrial democracy', and the Bullock Committee was appointed to examine and report on the preferred way ahead. It became fairly obvious that they were intending to recommend the adoption of worker directors on company boards. In West Germany we employed about 6,000 people, operating their system of having employee representatives on supervisory boards, and it worked well. But it worked in the special context of that country, conditioned by its history over the last hundred years, including tight trades union movement constraints, which would have been unacceptable in the UK. Also, in the UK our company was dealing with twenty-four unions, whereas in Germany we had one.

Nevertheless we decided to extend the scope of our consultative procedures, which had basically been focused on a broad range of personnel matters. The first step was to establish additional bodies at the division level for the division boards to have discussions with the representatives of both weekly and monthly staff about the business and investment policy. The final step was to establish a Central Business and Investment Committee (CBIC), chaired by Bill Duncan, an ICI deputy chairman, and supported by other directors with representatives of all the division CBIC's. These worked well and obviously filled a gap in our consultation procedures.

Many other companies, I know, felt our overall consultation arrangements were 'over the top' but the outcome was that for many years ICI did not have any serious industrial disputes or strikes. I believe the opportunity for employees' representatives at all levels to discuss their concerns and aspirations with their management, up to and including the ICI board, was a major contributor to this desirable outcome.

We equally endeavoured to develop the best possible relationships with our trade union leaders, including Len Murray, Hugh Scanlon, David Basnett, Frank Chappell, Johnny Miller and Clive Jenkins and their immediate lieutenants. Jim Bell, the general manager responsible for our weekly staff, headed our negotiating team with the unions and he was quite the best negotiator I have ever come across. We also enjoyed socializing with union colleagues.

Hugh Scanlon and Jack Jones had become probably the two most powerful union leaders in recent times during the Wilson government. Hugh became such a thorn in Wilson's side, that the Prime Minister once desperately ordered him: 'Get your tanks off my lawn!' Hugh and I became good friends and I found him a very engaging character. We had a series of golf matches with Jim Bell and one of Hugh's colleagues. Incidentally, although he was an occasional golfer like myself, Hugh could still play to a low handicap. If he had devoted his life to the game rather than the trade unions, I believe he could have been a successful professional golfer.

There was one memorable game when Hugh invited us to play on his home course at Broadstairs. We arrived at his house in a sea mist, with visibility no more than 50 yards. I said it was sad we would not be able to play, but Hugh quickly contradicted me, saying: 'We will be perfectly safe, as no one else will be daft enough to play.' We had played about half the round, when we arrived at a short hole. The four of us drove off, but when we reached the green there were six balls clearly visible! Then out of the mist two lady golfers suddenly emerged, having played off the ladies' tee. Even Hugh had to call it a day.

On another occasion Hugh paid quite a tribute to ICI, when he said that if the Amalgamated Engineering Union (AEU) had been seeking a source for a wider industrial dispute, ICI would be the last company they would pick. People frequently told me: 'You in ICI are very lucky – you never seem to have any strikes.' I usually bit my tongue and just reflected on Hugh's compliment.

When I made my maiden speech in the House of Lords on the subject of the manufacturing industry Hugh was the next speaker and said, 'I am sure the House will join me in congratulating Lord Haslam on his magnificent speech. I have had the pleasure of knowing him – perhaps crossing swords with him is a better way to put it – over the years. He brings to the House a unique record of knowledge and experience within the chemical, coal and steel industries, as well as long experience in industrial relations. We hope we shall receive many more contributions from him in the future.'

Another key element of my job was to advise the ICI board Appointments Committee on the development and selection of candidates for divisional director posts, senior head office jobs and the boards of our major overseas companies. The procedures for the UK were well developed when I became Personnel Director and I was anxious to build on the more embryonic situation internationally.

When I was Chairman of ICI Fibres, Dennis Cordiner joined us from ICI Australia as a deputy chairman. He and his brother had been among the all-time greats in Australian football. I was impressed by the impact he had on our affairs and the many new concepts he brought to the party. I believe these international movements generated a mutual understanding and respect which made a real contribution to our corporate strength.

My procedure was to visit every UK division and each major overseas company once a year to discuss their succession plans with all board members and to hear about emerging high flyers. Whenever possible I met the people we had been discussing. I was supported on my UK visits by Bill Stead, and overseas by Jack Coates, two of my closest and able general managers. On our return to Head Office we prepared a report on our deliberations, which was circulated to the ICI directors and subsequently acted as a backcloth for our discussions at the board's Appointments Committee. I spent a quarter of my time on these succession procedures. Arguably it was the most important part of my job because these were the people who were going to determine the success of the company over future decades – not only as a business enterprise and a creator of wealth for the communities in which we operated, but also as an eminent employer of people.

My role as Personnel Director came to an unexpected end in October 1979, when Maurice Hodgson asked me to move to the USA to become Territorial Director of the Americas. The background to this was that, following our acquisition of the Atlas Company, their chief executive, Ed Goett, had become Chairman of ICI Americas. CIL, our major Canadian subsidiary, and our companies in Latin America had also been asked to report to him. The senior non-executive directors in CIL had rebelled to this and come to London to express their displeasure. They had indicated they would resign unless CIL was able to report to the ICI board through a director, as in the past. This was the trigger for my move to the USA, with the clear understanding that the line of responsibility between the ICI Group companies in the USA, Canada and Latin America and the Main Board would be through me.

Phase 3. 1979–81

On moving to the USA, I was joined by Robin Biggam, who had been my finance director at ICI Fibres, and Rex Palmer, who had a strong planning background. I based our activities in New York and was quickly regarded as a local hero in Canada and Latin America but, understandably, with apprehension in ICI Americas' headquarters in Wilmington, because my role had removed some of their previous responsibilities.

My first visit to Wilmington, accompanying Ray Pennock, who was the ICI Deputy Chairman with responsibility for the Americas, did not get off to a propitious start. We had already acquired a VCM plant at Baton Rouge, the basic building block for PVC products. Plans were at an advanced stage to buy a major PVC pipe business, enabling us to build a PVC plant. This strategy had been approved by the Heavy Chemicals Product Group, headed by John Harvey-Jones and Jack Lofthouse, who had been my predecessor as Territorial Director. The strategy also had the provisional approval of the ICI board. This became the focal point of our visit and Ray asked me for my frank views on the project. I replied that I would not touch it with the proverbial barge-pole. Ray said he believed the ICI board should review the project once again. When they did, it was decided we should not proceed. This did not earn me any plaudits with my new ICI Americas colleagues.

Ed Goett, who had been Chief Executive of the Atlas Group, was a strong and effective leader and he carried these qualities into his new ICI role. But he made the mistake of trying to run his enlarged organization as a personal fiefdom, keeping ICI involvement, as far as possible at arm's length. He was also bitter that the verbal assurances he believed had been made during the takeover negotiations – that he would also assume responsibility for our Canadian and Latin American operations – were no longer being honoured. Inevitably, and with much regret, we came to the conclusion that we should seek his early retirement and Ray Pennock and I explained the situation to him. This was the most difficult such discussion of my whole career – particularly as I had a lingering doubt that promises had indeed been made to him which had not been honoured.

The situation was compounded by the fact that Bob Barnett, who was Ed Goett's deputy, had already announced his desire to retire early. So I had to work hard to persuade him to stay and become Chairman of ICI Americas. He agreed, and Harry Corless, who had had a distinguished ICI career in the UK, took over as his successor. My relationship with ICI Americas took an immediate turn for the better and Bob Barnett and I quickly developed a close and beneficial relationship.

George Whitby had made two major contributions to ICI before he retired in 1974, first in fibres and thereafter as Territorial Director for the Americas in the formative years. His vision was to build on our involvements in pharmaceuticals and speciality chemicals, and of course our highly successful partnership with American Celanese in fibres, of which he had been one of the prime architects. I shared this concept and persuaded the ICI board that our foray into heavy chemicals should be abandoned. We quickly sold off the VCM plant to the Taiwanese and our decision to abandon our PVC ambitions was quickly vindicated as we were offered five PVC businesses in the course of the next six months. However, we had also acquired a third share in a catalytic cracker plant at Corpus Christi and were in the process of building a glycol plant. We had great difficulty in selling these involvements in the global recession which then existed, but eventually they were also divested.

This experience in the USA underlined my feeling that ICI had suffered from backing a heavy chemical policy for too long and too intensively. The balance of the board in my time was dominated by directors from the heavy chemical divisions and indeed there was a spell when Alfred Spinks and I were the only directors with a different divisional pedigree.

George Whitby told me that in the late 1960s the dominant group of directors from the North-east continuously pressed for a large US acquisition based on heavy chemicals but he was adamant that he would not touch heavy chemicals in competition with the already large and successful companies. I was therefore faced with the task of having to reverse yet another wave of endeavours to establish a heavy chemical presence in the US. In retrospect I believe the ICI board during this period would have benefited from having a better balance of directors drawn from heavy chemicals and the remaining divisions.

Our pharmaceuticals business was already flourishing. The Pharmaceuticals Division was anxious to launch their new beta-blocker Tenormin in the USA and it was on the verge of approval from the Food and Drug Administration (FDA). This was a new world to me, but I blanched when the experts in both the UK and the USA confirmed we would need 1,000 representatives equipped with cars to market the drug. Having built up and trained this team, the FDA's approval was perversely delayed. It was decided, however, during this temporary lull that we should focus on a special campaign, linked to sharp television exposure, to sell the well established Mylanta products of Stewart Pharmaceuticals, which had been acquired in the Atlas deal. This campaign was remarkably successful and I believe nearly every medicine cabinet in the USA must have been full of Mylanta products. It certainly taught me a lesson about the power of television and an intensive marketing campaign.

We enjoyed an active social life in the USA, having the use of an apartment in the Olympic Tower next to St Patrick's Cathedral on Fifth Avenue, with our office in the same building. I had the shortest outdoor commute ever – just 30 yards separating my apartment lift from the office lift. We also rented two homes during our stay, both near Darien in Connecticut. We had moved home several times in the UK but always acquired an immediate family of ICI friends. On this occasion we had no immediate friends, with the notable exception of Allan and Jane Dragone, whom we had known well in our earlier involvements in ICI Plastics and ICI Fibres. What was extraordinary, however, was the way our new neighbours overwhelmed us with gracious hospitality. We were frequently invited to parties by people we had never even met.

The second house we rented on Long Island Sound was owned by Bill Roosevelt, the grandson of the former president. He left behind all his family scrapbooks and correspondence, which made fascinating reading. The house was on Nathan Hale Road and at a nearby cocktail party an old lady asked me if I felt it was appropriate for an English couple to be living in this road. I asked my host, 'What gives with Nathan Hale?' He explained that he was the eminent American who had spied on the British. Having sailed across to Long Island from the jetty next to our house, he was captured by the British and subsequently hanged on Manhattan, when he made the memorable farewell speech: 'My only regret is I have only one life to give to my country.'

Another unusual feature of my life in the USA was the number of times strangers in restaurants asked me if I was a member of the Churchill family – perhaps because at the time I weighed almost 4 stone more than now. One evening I had booked a table at Le Cirque Restaurant in New York and when I approached the *maître d'*, he spontaneously said, 'Mr Churchill, I have saved the best table in the house for you.' After a brief pause, I decided that I must come clean and explained I was not Mr Churchill, but Mr Haslam. He gave us the adjacent table, so we were able to observe the arrival of the 'real' Mr Churchill. He was about 5 feet tall and looked like a Mexican! The *maître d'* again expressed his regrets and explained that this was one of their problems, with people booking tables in false, high-sounding names.

Our visits to the Masters at Augusta National Golf Club were impressive. Peter Allen, in his ICI days, was the first non-American member, through his close friendship with Charlie Yates, who was the Secretary. Charlie was a renowned golfer, having been the US Amateur Champion in 1938 and leading amateur at the Masters on three occasions. Peter Allen and Consuelo, his wife, went to the Masters each year and invited Joyce and me to accompany them. We stayed in the prestigious Butler's Cabin, which was a real privilege as many of the eminent golfers would come there for a drink after completing their rounds.

One special occasion was a Sunday evening before the winner's dinner, when Tom Watson had won the Green Jacket. He and his family arrived for pre-dinner drinks at the Cabin and, with Charlie missing, Peter and I and our wives were temporary hosts. I was amazed that Tom, having done so many television interviews, was still living his last round stroke by stroke, and described it to Peter and me in precise detail.

The other privilege which Peter Allen enjoyed was to run his Mistresses competition on the Monday for a few friends. So I can claim to have played round Augusta in a recognized competition, and the highlight of my whole golfing career was making a two on the infamous twelfth hole.

Maurice Hodgson had indicated that having sorted out the organizational structure in the Americas, our most important task was to seek opportunities to expand ICI's activities, particularly in the USA. We had many functions at the New York 21 Club, where we entertained leaders of the major chemical and related industries and financial institutions. I was pleasantly surprised at how even the most senior people were happy to join us. Joyce and I were in turn invited by many companies to charity functions and there was rarely an evening when we were not out and about.

An epic function was the visit of the Prince of Wales in June 1981 to celebrate the fiftieth anniversary of the Royal Ballet at the Lincoln Center's Metropolitan Opera House. Unfortunately it was the time of the Bobby Sands affair, and *en route* to the Opera House we had to pass through crowds of threatening Irish agitators. The function was attended by Nancy Reagan and the upper crust of New York's society. Arriving at our seats, we felt that all was well – but far from it. Some of the IRA supporters and their wives had acquired tickets and come appropriately dressed. When the curtain was raised they dashed down the aisles throwing objects into the audience, which might have been bombs but were actually awful propaganda documents. I was enormously proud of the Royal Ballet Company, who continued to perform brilliantly when they must have been scared out of their wits! The police removed the protesters in a heavy-handed way; when I went to the men's loo at the interval, some were still lying on the floor bleeding!

Ray Pennock retired at the end of March 1980 to take up the chairmanship of BICC and also the presidency of the CBI, and the board appointed me, as Deputy Chairman, to be his successor. However, I was pleased that I was to continue to be based in the Americas, and there was no doubt the promotion helped the level of my acceptance on the US scene.

Another helpful factor was that our consul-general in New York was Gordon Booth, whom I had not met since we were schoolboys together in Bolton, and his wife Jeanne I had first met when I was three! Moreover, Michael Angus was my Unilever opposite number in New York; he was eventually to become Chairman of Unilever plc. We had occasional lunches together to share our experiences in penetrating the US market and discussing our mutual tax problems. Another friendly face was Bob Malpas, who had recently retired from ICI to join his long-standing friend Ralph Landau in running his Halcon Group. Bob was a brilliant lecturer and was heavily in demand on the New York circuit. On the odd occasion I was asked to speak, I asked whether Bob was on the same bill, if so I declined, as the contrast would be too stark. Bob usually made his presentation with a battery of projectors and flashing lights, whereas I could only muster five slides.

ICI's financial advisers were Goldman Sachs and Smith Barney, who were helpful in a rather pedestrian way. I met Bruce Wasserstein and Jeffrey Rosen, who were then with First Boston, and had far more helpful advice from them – surprisingly without any recompense, while we were paying our formal advisers an arm and a leg. However, as I say in Chapter 10, the pay-off to Bruce and Jeffrey came later!

By 1980 my team and I had decided to focus on two attractive acquisitions: Rohm & Haas and American Celanese Corporation. Unfortunately the timing could not have been worse, as there was a global downturn and in the first quarter of 1980 the ICI Group went into the red for the first time and had to cut its dividend.

We had exploratory discussions with Vince Gregory, then Chairman and CEO of Rohm & Haas, and one Monday I was to visit members of the Haas family to obtain their reactions. However, before I left our New York office, Maurice Hodgson rang me to say that the ICI executive directors had met that morning and, because of the difficult ICI financial situation, they felt I should not pursue this option any further.

We already had a close relationship with American Celanese through our partnership in Fibre Industries, and we held a series of discussions with John Macomber, the Chairman, and Allan Dragone, his number 2, about the possibility of ICI acquiring the whole company. We had tentatively worked out a potential valuation of about $1 billion – the exchange rate was then hovering about $2.40 to the pound, so we were talking about less than £500 million. However, before this proposition could be tested with the Celanese board, my ICI board colleagues expressed their unwillingness to support the deal, primarily because they were unhappy about increasing our involvement in the fibre operations. They did not recognize that Celanese would have opened up new market opportunities such as paints. Hoescht eventually bought the company for $2.4 billion.

In contrast to these disappointments over acquisitions, our ICI Americas core businesses – pharmaceuticals, polyester fibre, urethanes, agricultural chemicals, catalysts, specialities and resins – continued to expand and flourish.

CIL, our Canadian subsidiary, was a producer of agricultural and industrial chemicals, paints, plastics, industrial explosives and mining equipment. It was headed by Bill Mandry and had a renowned group of non-executive directors, most of them chairmen of major Canadian corporations. I attended the CIL board meetings to keep in touch with their progress, and the company steamed ahead with the minimum of demands on me. In this difficult year of 1980 CIL sales were up 14 per cent and profits up 3.4 per cent over the previous year. We decided on an important strategy: increasingly to ignore the border between the USA and Canada. For example, we decided to use CIL in Alberta as a base for attacking the US alkali and fertilizer market. Conversely we were also developing supplies to Canada of pharmaceuticals from the USA.

An unusual problem was the difficulty we had in moving management people and their families into Montreal, the location of our head office, because of the Francophone policies being pursued, particularly in education. So we took the difficult decision to move our headquarters to Toronto. Despite heavy pressures from the Quebec government, we went ahead, and the anticipated benefits quickly followed.

Every few months I had meetings with all the heads of our Latin American countries, Mexico or Rio being our normal venues. Only three of these countries had substantial manufacturing operations – Argentina, Brazil and Mexico – the others primarily marketing ICI's imported products. They were mainly managed by local nationals, although Brazil was creditably led by an expatriate, John Matthews. The outstanding performer, however, was Tom Hudson, who initially chaired our Mexican operation but returned to his native Buenos Aires to run our Argentina business.

In midsummer 1981, Maurice Hodgson said he believed it would be desirable for me to return to the UK and 'throw my hat in the ring' in the exercise which would shortly commence to find his successor. I had mixed feelings about leaving the USA, as I had hoped to achieve more, particularly on acquisitions. However, I was pleased that yet again Brian Smith was taking over my Territorial Director role, as we usually shared the same ideas. Also, in my Deputy Chairman role, I would still have an overview of our Americas interests.

The last two years had been a great experience for Joyce and me.

Our family, too, had benefited from holidaying at least twice a year in the USA or Canada, and in any case they were also seeing us when we visited the UK every few weeks. So the announcement of our return to the UK was not received with total joy. With considerable reluctance we handed over our rented house in Nathan Hale Road to Brian and Phyllis Smith.

Phase 4. 1981–3

When I returned to the UK at the end of September the press were already building up a head of steam about the 'ICI Chairman Stakes'. A typical comment appeared in *Chemical Business*:

> Now, it is said, the choice is between three deputy chairmen: all change in the form of the outspoken, colourful and controversial John Harvey-Jones; no change in the shape of politically adept but often abrasive Bill Duncan, who has a hold on the most important committees at board level; and some change in the guise of a dark horse, Bob Haslam, now returning from the USA who is quiet and conventional.
>
> At this stage, there is no knowing which of the three will be chosen. Many believe Bill Duncan to be the front-runner, though he would not be the most popular choice within the company. Many fear that the Harvey-Jones form of radicalism would be too uncomfortable, that the group is not yet prepared to face such an upheaval. And others feel that the choice will fall on Mr Haslam, the compromise candidate.

The reality was that I had only been a deputy chairman briefly, and had been based in the USA, where I was 'out of sight and out of mind'. There were past examples of ICI directors who had vacated Millbank for a period and had subsequently missed out on the chairmanship – a classic case was Dick Beeching, who chaired British Rail with distinction. He must have had expectations of becoming the ICI chairman soon after his return, but it did not happen.

The procedure for appointing a new chairman was that the senior non-executive director – in this case Arnold Hall, then Chairman of Hawker Siddeley – canvassed each director individually, asking each: 'If you are not to become chairman yourself, who would be your first and second choice?' He then passed on his soundings to the Chairman. As some reporters mocked, the only feature missing was that there were no smoke signals coming out of Millbank!

During my time in the USA I met board members of all the leading chemical companies. With the exception of Du Pont and Dow Chemicals, I believe the calibre of my ICI colleagues was superior to that of their US counterparts. Nevertheless the US businesses were better run because their directors were more 'hands-on' executives, as compared with our more ambassadorial style. This view was also reinforced in my chats with Mike Angus about how Unilever organized their board.

I had decided to back Bill Duncan because I believed we shared much the same view as to how the board could be slimmed down and made more executive, although my views were probably more extreme than his.

The outcome of the election process was that the board elected John Harvey-Jones as the next Chairman. ICI was regarded as British industry's school for top management. The average tenure of the Chairman was about four years, the notable exception being Harry McGowan who reigned for twenty-one years. Every time the company appointed a new chairman, the retiring incumbent and the unsuccessful deputy chairmen tended to fly off to new pastures, providing ready-trained chairmen for companies who were not so good at producing their own. So it was obvious that the press would immediately focus on what would happen to Bill Duncan and myself.

Bill was understandably depressed by the outcome of the selection process. He withdrew somewhat from his vigorous involvement in ICI affairs and focused on seeking an appropriate chairmanship elsewhere. In November 1982 he moved to Rolls-Royce Ltd in preparation for taking over as Chairman. As I had only recently returned from the USA, I did not have any expectations that I would be chosen. However, my future was clear from the outset. I had joined Tate & Lyle as a non-executive director in 1978 and while in the USA I had been Chairman of Tate & Lyle Inc. On returning to the UK George Jellicoe, then Chairman of Tate & Lyle, suggested to me that if I did not become ICI chairman, he would be delighted if I would succeed him at a timing of my choosing. I felt, however, that it would be inappropriate to leave ICI and the new Chairman immediately, so I became a non-executive deputy chairman of Tate & Lyle and took over from George in April 1983.

When I was Chairman of ICI Fibres, John Harvey-Jones was Chairman of the Petrochemicals Division. As they were suppliers of most of our raw materials, it was essential that we had a very close working relationship. In those days the prices at which products moved internally from one division to another were the generators of much heated argument, as obviously they had a significant impact on the apparent profitability of each division. I must pay tribute to John for the balanced and fair way he reacted, and we could not have had a better relationship. There was no doubt that he was a fine chairman of his division and fully deserved his early elevation to the ICI board.

The year I spent with him as ICI Chairman had some trying moments. He was widely sought after as a speaker. Each speech he made was well based – he often showed the text to me and it could not be faulted. The trouble arose in the discussions which followed, as John could not resist a rather dramatic throw-away response, which was all part of his flamboyant style and it served him so well in his subsequent TV career. A classic example of this was a speech he made in Frankfurt. Afterwards he was asked: 'What is the single most important thing that could happen to put the UK economy back on its way to recovery?' He replied: 'The removal of Mrs Thatcher.' Within an hour our PR team and I were being bombarded by the media asking if this was ICI board's considered formal view. The Prime Minister never forgave him for this and as many government officials were aware of her views, it tended to sour our wider relationship with the Government.

Fulfilling his promise to have even more consensus strategic discussions and objectives he initiated large meetings, not only of the ICI board and the UK division chairmen but also of the chairmen of our major overseas operations. These tended to be informalish meetings, and were too large and discursive to have a serious decision-making role.

John was a very complex character – full of charm, very fast on his feet, a radical thinker, but sometimes lacking in consistency. For example, with his earlier ICI background he had always been a supporter of a heavy chemical policy in developments overseas, but almost overnight switched and became an avid supporter of speciality chemicals and pharmaceuticals. He would then distance himself from the past mistakes we had made, as in the USA.

When Bill Duncan and I retired from the board, John indicated that this would enable him to reduce its size and develop a tighter style of management. Bill and I would have probably have followed this path, but with a key difference: it was not just a question of numbers but more importantly of behaviour, so that individual directors should become executively responsible for the global developments and performance of their product groups.

7
Tate & Lyle: 1982–6

When George Jellicoe became Chairman of Tate & Lyle in 1978 he was the first non-family member to assume this role. He took over at a time when profits had collapsed from £40 million to £25 million. I joined as non-executive Deputy Chairman in 1982 and succeeded George at the board's request in March 1983 on my retirement from ICI. George in turn became Chairman of the British Overseas Trade Board but helpfully agreed to continue to serve on the Tate & Lyle board.

George was one of the finest men I have ever worked with. He had a remarkably distinguished political and military career – his exceptional wartime record in the SAS led him to be showered with honours: DSO, MC, Legion d'Honeur, Croix de Guerre and Czech War Cross. He had an incredible range of international contacts and friends and I had the impression that no overseas prime minister visiting London failed to contact him. Nevertheless, this was the first time he had chaired an industrial company. He wisely invited a number of high-powered industrialists to join the board – Alex Alexander, Dick Cave and Fraser Sedcole – and they certainly made a significant impact in restoring Tate & Lyle's fortunes. Above all George Jellicoe was an immensely warm and generous man, and when he was around humour was never far away.

Probably his most definitive decision was inviting Neil Shaw, who was already on the board in his capacity as Chairman of the group's

Canadian subsidiary, Redpath, to move to London as Group Managing Director. I pay tribute to Saxon Tate, Neil's predecessor, for the gracious way he continued to serve effectively as a non-executive director on the board which he originally joined in 1956.

From the outset Neil and I had an ideal relationship and it was a pleasure to work with him. He was the most highly motivated executive I have known. George Jellicoe had improved the profits of the company year by year from the low point of 1978 and I was determined to maintain this progress. In the early days of our relationship Neil was already anxious to embark on a fairly ambitious acquisition programme but our 'treasure chest' was still too low, so for once in my life I was having to restrain rather than encourage my closest lieutenant!

Nevertheless, we continued to reshape the company away from its dependence on volatile commodity trading, which in 1979 had generated more than half the profits, so that in 1984 75 per cent came from manufacturing in the UK and North America. We also focused on improving productivity, tightening our management structure and modernizing the Thames refinery.

The executive directors were a commendable team. Frank Thomlinson was a powerful production director, Michael Attfield our internationally renowned trading director, and John Mitchell led our US group. Our Vice-Chairman, James Forbes, masterminded the group's finances over a particularly difficult five-year period and his final achievement was to oversee a rights issue, which raised £42 million.

With this rights money under our belt and the steadily increasing cash flow from the existing business, we were able to contemplate expanding our horizons in North America and Europe. An early acquisition was Alcantara, a major sugar company in Portugal, followed later by a second Portuguese sugar purchase, Sores, and we became a dominant and profitable player in this attractive market.

In this period our Canadian subsidiary, Redpath, acquired Donlee Manufacturing Industries, which supplied plastic parts to the motor industry as well as precision components for the nuclear and defence industries. This was a major step in Redpath's efforts to develop its non-sugar business in new growth areas. Negotiations led eventually to the sale to the Belize government of our controlling interest in Belize

Sugar Industries but we retained a long-term management contract with the Belizean industry.

We already had similar contracts to manage the Royal Swaziland Sugar Corporation and the Zambian Sugar Co, where a rather embarrassing situation emerged in early 1984. Our team in Zambia were paid primarily in sterling into their UK bank accounts, but we had not been recompensed by the Zambian government for over six months. I asked David Tate, who was then managing director of our Zambian operation, to inform President Kaunda, with whom he had a good relationship, that if we did not get paid, we would withdraw our team. This led to the President inviting Neil Shaw and me to visit Lusaka for discussions with him and his colleagues. We flew at night with Zambian Airways – not the best preparation for what was lying ahead. The flight arrived late, so instead of having a brief rest at our hotel, we were whisked off directly to State House and escorted into a large room where nearly all the TV cameras in Zambia were assembled. Kaunda entered and made a pleasant welcoming speech, to which I had to respond spontaneously. He then led us into the dining room, for lunch with him and many of his cabinet ministers. He explained during the meal that he would have to leave soon to place a wreath on the memorial in honour of their fallen freedom fighters and added: 'It is rather like your Whitehall Ceremony, but on a smaller scale!' He would return, however, to participate in our opening discussions.

That evening we were having a quiet drink with David and Jenny Tate at their home, and switched on the TV to watch how our event had been reported. First on the news, the commentator said the President has been talking to Mr Haslam of 'Tattie & Lillie' today about the future of the Zambian sugar industry, but the visual on the screen was a shot of the President's backside, as he laid a wreath at the memorial. A blare of martial music followed, with the commentator reporting that the President has been honouring the freedom fighters today, but on the screen was a shot of Neil and me presenting an antique sugar bowl to him. I am sure Kaunda must have been livid, as over lunch he was praising the minister responsible for their media activities as really outstanding.

After three days negotiating with the President and his colleagues we agreed a satisfactory debt repayment programme, which commendably they honoured. However, they had little option as, after copper, sugar was their second major export. During discussions we broke off from time to time to have drinks or meals with various members of the British community and only had to enter a room for our fellow guests to start applauding the 'freedom fighters'!

During the family reign Tate & Lyle had owned many of the sugar plantations in Jamaica, but they were all eventually nationalized by the Jamaican government. However, under local management they deteriorated dramatically and the position arose where the World Bank would not provide further finance unless Tate & Lyle personnel returned to resume management of the operation. We took up this challenge but it involved asking retired senior managers to return to their former plantations. They were all very distressed to see how quickly the operation had gone downhill.

Joyce and I visited Jamaica to thank our colleagues and at the largest plantation much admired what our people were achieving in restoring its fortunes. A surprising feature was that a small café had been established in the centre of the plantation and, alarmingly, drugs were being sold and consumed there.

In earlier days the Tate and Lyle families had a lovely home on the plantation as a holiday retreat. In honour of our visit the local government people decided to invite a number of dignitaries to join us for lunch and reopened the house for this purpose. Fortunately it went off very well despite the fact that many of the services in the house were no longer working – and we had to wash our hands in buckets brought from afar. One guest was the local chief of police and I asked him if he was aware of the café and its activities and why no action was being taken. He confirmed that he knew but said it was located a long way from the main road, and his police did not have enough petrol to make regular forays to the café to investigate what was taking place!

In 1984, as our financial position continued to improve, we were able to contemplate making more ambitious acquisitions and decided that Brooke Bond would be an attractive target to add to our existing tea and sugar activities. Neil Shaw and I visited a very surprised John Cuckney, the Chairman of Brooke Bond, to inform him of our intentions. As the bid progressed there were strong indications that, in the absence of a counter-bidder, we would succeed in acquiring the company at an acceptable price. We had anticipated that Unilever might enter the fray, which they eventually did at a price 20 per cent above our offer and 60 per cent above the Brooke Bond share price immediately prior to our bid. We still hoped the Unilever bid might be turned down by the Monopolies Commission but it was not to be. We had some compensation for our efforts, however, our shareholding yielding a profit of nearly £1 million.

We had two surprise visits from distinguished guests in 1984. First, the Lay Assistant of the Archbishop of Canterbury, Robert Runcie, rang up to suggest that we might invite him to lunch. Some quick research showed that the Archbishop's father had spent most of his working life as the electrical engineer at our Liverpool refinery and Tate & Lyle had supported his son financially during his Oxford days. It turned out to be a delightful lunch. In his few remarks the Archbishop said his father was often out of their home in the evenings, occasionally dealing with electrical problems at the refinery. His father had given him enough problem-solving advice for him to respond immediately with a likely solution. But the comment we particularly welcomed was when the Archbishop said: 'If my father, as I expect, is now looking down on this scene, he will be much prouder that I am lunching with the Tate & Lyle board than he ever was when I became the Archbishop of Canterbury!'

The second visit followed a call from the office of the Lord Mayor Elect, Sir Alan Traill, who wished to move the traditional fireworks display following the Lord Mayor's Show from the vicinity of the then GLC headquarters much closer to Tower Bridge, and that the Sugar Quay terrace would be an ideal viewing point. E.D. & F. Man and ourselves, who shared the building, readily accepted and we were delighted to entertain the Lord Mayor and Lady Mayoress and their entourage on this special occasion.

In May 1984 James Kerr Muir joined the board as Finance Director and in September he was joined by L.R. (Red) Wilson, who had presided over our Canadian interests since 1981. His appointment reflected the increasing importance of North America in the group's future, and soon he masterminded our activities across the Continent. I had always hoped that he would be the natural successor to Neil Shaw, but his family were reluctant to relocate to the UK. Eventually, when he retired from the group, he served with distinction in a series of top roles in Canadian banking.

Another welcome board appointment in 1985 was Jane Prior as the first female non-executive director in the group's history. She quickly surprised all her colleagues by a vigorous round of visits to group locations and rapidly demonstrated her value on the board by making a quite unique contribution.

Tate & Lyle also developed a talent for producing bright young politicians, the two most prominent recently being David Davis, who became Chairman of the Conservative Party and is Shadow deputy prime minister, and Colin Moynihan, who had a ministerial career and was a Conservative front-bench spokesman in the House of Lords.

In 1985 the group made its first major investments since the late 1970s with a heavy focus on North America. Our molasses business purchased the Speciality Feeds Division of A. E. Staley, and also acquired the much larger Agri-Products Division from Beatrice Inc. Unitank Terminal Service purchased a bulk terminal facility at the Port of San Francisco, enabling the group to offer facilities in all the major US ports. Our major acquisition was the purchase of Hunt Bros' sugar interests in the Midwest, comprising six beet sugar factories. The business was in receivership at the time and production of beet – the staple farm product of the area – faced total collapse. Our intervention revitalized the industry and secured the future of the local beet farmers. We named the operation the Western Sugar Company.

On retiring from Tate & Lyle in February 1986, I was pleased to report that I had been able to extend George Jellicoe's legacy to the group, having increased profits year by year for the seventh year. The year I took over the profit had been £40 million and by 1985 this had nearly doubled to £77 million and the return on capital was over 21 per cent.

People often asked me how I could chair two such very different businesses as sugar and steel at the same time, not having been involved before in either industry. The answer was, 'With difficulty.' The basic reason was that the two companies had outstanding chief executives in Neil Shaw and Bob Scholey. Nevertheless, it was still difficult because every day I was in London I would normally be at British Steel in the morning and move to Tate & Lyle in the afternoon. Though the businesses could not have been more different in character, both companies had able and high-calibre people. There was never any hope of achieving the professionalism of those who had been in a single business all their working lives, and so it was essential to discern quickly those close colleagues whose views carried the most weight. At the same time I had to inject my own ideas into the decision-making process in the hope that this would provide an added beneficial dimension. Organizations, however successful, can be somewhat inbred and for this reason welcome an injection of new thinking and ideas into their affairs.

My first objective at both companies was to get to know quickly at least 100 senior members of the teams. But this could have its embarrassing repercussions. One Saturday morning while walking around Harrods I met one of our young executives, but could not decide whether he worked for Tate & Lyle or British Steel. As no clarity emerged from our conversation, I decided that he had made a presentation to me on the potential for steel manufacture in Morocco, so in desperation I queried 'How are things in Morocco?' He replied, 'I don't really know as I have just returned from my honeymoon in Torquay, and incidentally I work for Tate & Lyle.' This really put me in my place!

To sum up, my brief spell at Tate & Lyle was probably the most enjoyable of my varied industrial career. Arriving there daily from British Steel was like visiting a a quiet haven. Board members and senior management generated a great sense of support and warmth, and this seemed to permeate the whole operation. Industrial and human relations were of a high order and although in business terms the group performance had declined during the final period of the family leadership, nevertheless I believe those of us who followed benefited from the enviable personnel relationships they had cultivated.

Among other involvements during this period was membership of the British Overseas Trade Board in 1981–5, under the chairmanship of the Duke of Kent. I was particularly pleased when he asked me to chair its North America Advisory Group, as it enabled me to sustain my interest in the US and Canadian markets.

In 1982 Peter Carey and I were asked to become the government directors of the newly privatized Cable & Wireless operation. This gave me an insight into yet another exciting industry under the lively chairmanship of Eric Sharp, a colleague dating back to my ICI Fibres days.

8
British Steel: 1983–6

In June 1983 Peter Carey, then Permanent Secretary at the Department of Trade and Industry, rang me and humorously said he understood I was relatively unemployed, as I was only 50 per cent engaged at Tate & Lyle! Would I therefore be interested in becoming part-time chairman of British Steel in succession to Ian MacGregor. My immediate reaction was to say no, because it seemed to me the job demanded a full-time commitment and I could not leave Tate & Lyle. However, Bob Scholey, who was Chief Executive of British Steel Corporation (BSC), came to see me. He said in his usual forthright way, 'I should be chairman but I am not going to be, so please come, as I know we will work well together.' Knowing that I would have two very able chief executives in Neil Shaw and Bob Scholey, I rang Peter Carey and accepted. It provided me with a classic opportunity to compare the administration of a nationalized industry and a private-sector operation. It was to be a fascinating period.

I knew that I had been the second choice as Alistair Frame, then Chairman of RTZ, had been approached and appeared to be accepting. But word of his candidacy got out prematurely, before he had discussed it with his board, so he turned down the offer. Recognizing this sensitivity, Margaret Thatcher subsequently wrote to the Tate & Lyle board thanking them for the helpful way they had reacted to my future involvement in BSC.

Patrick Jenkin was the Secretary of State at the time of my appointment but when I took up the post on 1 September, he had been replaced in a Cabinet reshuffle by Cecil Parkinson, who gave me tough objectives for British Steel:

(1)   To achieve break-even before interest in 1984/5 and freedom from state aid in 1986/7

(2)   To bring the cost structure of BSC's businesses into line with that of their principal European competitors and, where necessary, to dispose of businesses and plants which were unable, in the longer term, to meet this criterion

(3)   To privatize BSC as quickly as practicable, with priority being given to those areas of business which overlapped with the private sector and with activities outside the mainstream BSC steel businesses.

In 1976 when Charles Villiers had taken over as Chairman from his predecessor Monty Finniston, he had inherited a rapid expansion programme which was designed to increase the liquid steel capacity from 20 to 30 million tons per year, when sales actually began falling. This called for drastic action. Eventually Charles and Bob Scholey arranged a day-long conference at Blacknest, Charles' home on the edge of Windsor Great Park, which produced this blueprint for the future:

- To cut the target for liquid steel capacity from 30 to 15 million tons per annum
- To start giving effect to this forthwith, by closing old plants
- To face Government with the prospect of heavy redundancies.

I believe this was a defining moment in the future of BSC.

On his retirement in 1980 *The Economist* wrote unfairly that only Villiers was allowed access to capital to construct new steel works. This was too much for Charles and he replied:

In my time at BSC we cancelled the doubling of Port Talbot, arc furnaces at Hunterston and a plate mill at Teesside. We finished four schemes already begun, but we closed Clyde Iron Works and steel making at Hartlepool, Cardiff, Ebbw Vale, Shelton, Bilston, Glengarnock, Hallside, Corby, Shotton and Consett. We mothballed half the steel works at Port Talbot and Llanwern. We cut capacity by 50 per cent and took decisions which made 70,000 of the workforce redundant. I was not a steel plant builder, but the Chairman who had to do the dreadful spadework.

The distressing consequences in the communities lying in the areas of the closed or mothballed steel plants had been recognized by Monty Finniston, who belatedly set up an embryonic organization to create alternative job opportunities. Villiers built vigorously on this initiative and it was eventually launched as British Steel (Industry) (BSI). MacGregor commendably asked Villiers, after he ceased to be Chairman of BSC, to continue as Chairman of BSI. Equally impressed by what Villiers had achieved, I was delighted when he continued in this role during my time. Over the twelve years he was Chairman of BSI, Villiers claimed he had supported over 3,000 companies, which led to the creation of over 95,000 new job opportunities in steel locations.

Charles Villiers handed over the chairmanship of BSC to Ian MacGregor in 1980, with the restructuring plan well under way. In his final year the trading loss was £350 million, but because of the impact of the restructuring activities, total losses had risen to £1.7 billion, primarily because exceptional items, including writing off redundant assets and making redundancy payments, accounted for over £1.4 billion. This perverse feature, I believe, disguised the real achievements of Villiers. Unfortunately, in the final period of his chairmanship his relationship with Bob Scholey had become somewhat acrimonious, and this led to the Conservative government bringing in MacGregor as his successor.

From the outset MacGregor and Scholey established a good working relationship and they accelerated the restructuring. During MacGregor's period the trading loss was reduced to £275 million and the total loss to £869 million. Manpower reductions were running at the highest level and productivity rapidly improved.

The European Commission recognized in 1980 that an internecine war was breaking out between European steel producers, primarily because each country would support its own steel industry to avoid major losses of employment opportunities. This would certainly endanger the community spirit needed if the integration of Europe, so much desired by Brussels, was not to be snuffed out by a trade war over steel. Vicomte Davignon was made Commissioner for Industry and was successful in checking this development by persuading the companies concerned to reduce their steel capacities, and by bullying their governments into reducing the steel companies' subsidies, which made possible uneconomic production.

This involved setting up a European steel cartel, Eurofer. Capacity reductions were prescribed for all major products and production quotas were established. BSC suffered because the quotas were based on levels which corresponded to the earlier steel strike, when its production was artificially depressed. BSC adopted these edicts on a Queensbury Rules basis, but the French and Italians were unreliable performers. Even in my chairmanship the Italians were still building new steel plants in southern Italy at a time when we were shutting UK capacity on a major scale.

In the early days of Eurofer Villiers remonstrated with Davignon that the British were the only people who stuck to the agreements. 'You are the best boy in the class,' responded Davignon, who went on to say: 'Well we know we cannot and will not keep the agreements, but we do the best we can and that is better than doing nothing.' Nevertheless, with all its imperfections, it was generally agreed that Eurofer had been worthwhile and should continue. I wish I had been at an early Eurofer meeting when there was a lot of special pleading by governments and companies, and Bob Scholey electrified the session by his comment: 'What's the French for bullshit?' which echoed round the room, as he had forgotten to switch off his international translator.

When I arrived at BSC as Chairman Elect, I was well aware that MacGregor was not happy about me succeeding him and hence that relationship would not be easy. He made little effort to help the transition.

I was not unduly worried, except that discussions about BSC supplying steel slabs to US Steel were at their height and, indeed, MacGregor was expounding in the media almost daily on the subject. I repeatedly asked him to introduce me to David Roderick, the Chairman of US Steel, but he clearly had no intention of doing so. After his departure, I was even more surprised to find that Bob Scholey and Jake Stewart, the director responsible for our strip products, were no longer involved in the discussions. Bob Scholey advised that we should abandon the discussions forthwith but I responded that it would be impossible to do this in the first few days of my chairmanship, recognizing the head of steam which my predecessor had built up on this project. Fortunately Scholey and I were immediately to attend an International Iron and Steel Institute (IISI) conference in Vienna at which Roderick and his colleagues would also be present, so we got together. This gave us a clear picture of the point that they perceived the proposals had reached. They expressed some concern about the deal, which they put at a 50:50 prospect and we, too, outlined our reservations. It was agreed that discussions would continue to 'define and refine' the project and hopefully make the final decision before the end of the year. In December both boards discussed the outcome of these final proposals and came to the conclusion that we should not proceed because mutually beneficial terms could not be concluded. It was stressed that the decision had been taken purely on financial and business considerations and had not been influenced by political or other pressures. When the decision was taken at the BSC board meeting it was unanimous, including MacGregor, who had remained as a non-executive director. I particularly sought his view but he did not demur from his colleagues' decision. Nevertheless, this left the future of the Ravenscraig plant in Scotland uncertain.

Sadly, my relationship with Cecil Parkinson as Secretary of State was relatively short-lived as we had established a sound supportive working relationship. Unfortunately, in October the news of his affair with Sara Keays broke. Bob Scholey and I were due to see him that very evening and we both expected the meeting to be cancelled, but having received no such message we went along to the Victoria Street office, fully expecting he would not be there. We arrived to see the entrance surrounded by television cameras. Cecil was waiting for us as we stepped out of the lift. He said, 'I don't know about you chaps, but

I feel like a drink', and a bottle of whisky was immediately produced.

Cecil, in his book *Right at the Centre,* described the occasion concisely: 'On the Wednesday evening, I had my final ministerial meeting at 6 p.m. during which we agreed the external financial limit of BSC with Chairman, Bob Haslam.' I was full of admiration that he could focus on this topic with all his immediate problems – even in normal times this was not the most uplifting subject. For once I was pinching myself and thinking that this was not happening.

As we left, Michael Portillo, then his special adviser, joined Cecil to assist in drafting the speech he was to deliver to the Conservative Party conference at Blackpool next day. He subsequently offered his resignation, which I understand Margaret Thatcher accepted with great reluctance. Norman Tebbit took over as our Secretary of State and we quickly developed a first-class relationship. This was very timely as the build-up to the miners' strike was already beginning.

A strike had been widely expected from the moment Arthur Scargill became President of the National Union of Mineworkers (NUM) in 1981. For Scargill it was to be the dawn of a revolution. He believed that a sympathetic strike would begin in the 'socialist republic of South Yorkshire' and would spread like a fire across the nation, bringing down the Thatcher government, as his predecessor had brought down Heath's in 1974. The reality was different. His refusal to hold a strike ballot was widely condemned and his mass picketing tactics brought mass policing.

At that time of the NUM strike the steel workers were part of a triple alliance with the miners and the railway workers, but when the strike commenced the steel workers refused to follow the rail unions in supporting the miners. BSC installations and the pits manned by the members of the new Union of Democratic Miners (UDM), who continued working, became the prime targets for Scargill's violent flying pickets. In contrast the power stations were only mildly picketed, because miners' wives told them: 'You can picket where you like but don't go near those power stations, if you expect hot baths and cooked meals when you return home!'

Bill Sirs, the steelworkers' leader, defiantly declared: 'I am not here to see the steel industry crucified on someone else's altar.' I do not believe that the courageous role played by the leaders of the Iron and Steel Trades Confederation was ever fully appreciated. If they had combined with the miners and the railway workers under their triple alliance agreement, it would almost certainly have led to a near general strike – the car, food, and other engineering industries would quickly have ground to a halt. I believe their role deserved equal praise with the well-earned accolades which were showered on Roy Lynk and his working UDM miners during the strike.

One of our major problems was to deliver supplies of imported iron ore and coking coal to our major inland steel plants at Llanwern, Ravenscraig and Scunthorpe. This involved mounting massive convoys of lorries, carrying up to 300,000 tons a day to these plants, and this led to one particularly massive confrontation: the Battle of Orgreave Coke Works. Scargill mounted a blockade with over 6,000 violent pickets to prevent supplies reaching our Scunthorpe plant. This was the last straw as far as we were concerned and I rang Norman Tebbit to say that we wished to sue the NUM for totally ignoring the Conservatives' much-vaunted new employment laws, which limited the number of pickets to six. He was obviously sympathetic but said he would have to raise it at the next Cabinet meeting. Sadly, the Cabinet demurred. The first question put to Margaret Thatcher at her next radio interview was: 'Why are the chairmen of your nationalized industries not using your new labour laws about picketing?' She replied, 'I do not know. I do not understand it.' I rang Tebbit and expressed my displeasure. However I learned that on the following Tuesday, the Queen spoke to the Prime Minister about concerns regarding the use of police horses to control the pickets, and this led to a further Cabinet discussion. Tebbit then informed me that we could go ahead but we needed the agreement of Walter Marshall of the Central Electricity Generating Board (CEGB), Bob Reid of British Rail and Ian MacGregor of the National Coal Board (NCB). Bob Scholey and I met all our colleagues in these sister industries, but none of them would support us, in view of the dire consequences it might have on their affairs. So Margaret Thatcher was proved right. Miraculously, we were able to keep all our plants operating, thanks to the courageous efforts of the steelworkers and the lorry drivers, who were exposed to all kinds of physical violence, including concrete blocks being thrown down on them from motorway bridges.

There were amusing distractions, even in these daunting times. One evening we were entertaining Norman Tebbit to dinner when a surprising message came through that the 300 lorry drivers who were charged with the gruelling task of delivering supplies from Port Talbot to Llanwern in South Wales had held a meeting. Although they were happy with their accommodation and dining facilities at the Port Talbot works, they insisted we should provide a brothel there, so that they could unwind at the journey's end. Otherwise they might withdraw their labour! Norman said that obviously this was a management decision! However, next morning he rang me and said rather anxiously, 'You are not going to agree are you?' and cautioned that the tabloid press would have headlines like 'British Steel opens a brothel at Port Talbot with government stamp of approval'. This he believed would do neither him nor me any good! We had, however, already decided to take no action.

There were minor skirmishes when other unions held sympathy strikes with the miners. Some were deliberately contrived but had minimal impact. The most significant strike centred on Hunterston, our supply port for Ravenscraig's needs, where TGWU dockers indicated that they would not handle the next ship to arrive, the *Ostia*. We decided to use our own employees and if we had not done so the Ravenscraig plant would have closed. Norman Tebbit and the Government agreed to this provocative act and, as expected, it led to a national dock strike. As we had predicted, however, it had a minimal and short-lived impact.

Through the combined ingenuity and determination of the management and the workforce, BSC were able to stay in business and, more importantly, to maintain supplies to its UK and key export customers. The reaction of all our employees and their dedication to keeping their works operating were most heartening and praiseworthy. Nevertheless, the strike cost BSC £180 million, at a time when we could ill afford it. Even more important, it was a serious burden and distraction for senior management, when we were still heavily engaged in restructuring and improving the productivity and cost structures of our industry.

Prime Minister Thatcher had indicated she would not formally consult directly with the chairmen of nationalized industries during the strike. However, Joyce and I were invited to Number 10 on a number of occasions with me wearing my Tate & Lyle hat, and she always took the opportunity to have an informal chat about our difficulties in keeping the steel mills in production. I found these brief talks reassuring, as she was clearly well informed and appreciative of our problems.

In October at the Conservative Party conference at Brighton, the ghastly terrorist bomb outrage occurred, seriously injuring Norman Tebbit and his wife Margaret, who suffered even more devastating injuries. We in BSC were extremely distressed about this, as Norman was an outstanding secretary of state in supporting our endeavours at an exceptionally difficult time in our history. Despite the perception of him as tough and aggressive, I cannot remember having a row with him.

I received a letter from Margaret Thatcher asking me, during Norman's indisposition, to report to Norman Lamont, then the Minister for Industry at the Department of Trade and Industry (DTI), and so we kept moving along with our plans. However, in early December, I received a request from Callum McCarthy, then a DTI under-secretary who was living temporarily at Stoke Mandeville Hospital looking after the Tebbits' needs. The gist of the request was for me to visit Norman in hospital. On arrival I was amazed to find that I was not just there as a sick visitor, but that he had a brief about BSC's current problems which he wished to discuss. Although it was a few weeks since the bomb, he still looked very fragile and I deliberately avoided mentioning anything which was contentious. Nevertheless, he said as I left: 'If you have any serious problems, you come here!' Fortunately, in January 1985 he returned to his office in Victoria Street and normal business was resumed.

In the 1985 New Year's Honours List I received a knighthood, to the great pleasure of Joyce and myself and our family. At the Palace ceremony in February, the Queen, who had recently been on an overseas visit, involving shaking hands with thousands of well-wishers, had her right hand bandaged. She was clearly having difficulty handling the heavy sword and when it was my turn, instead of a tap on each shoulder there were two quite sharp blows, and instinctively I raised my hands to my ears. The Queen responded with a smile: 'No need to worry, they are still there!'

In April 1985 two other special events occurred. A successful modernization of the Hot Strip Mill at Port Talbot was completed and we invited the Prince and Princess of Wales to perform the opening ceremony. Soon after the date had been fixed, Peter Ashmore, then the Master of the Queen's Household, rang inviting my wife and me to join the Queen and other members of the Royal Family at Windsor Castle for what was normally referred to in the media as 'bed and breakfast' – but the Queen, I believe, preferred the expression 'dine and sleep'. Embarrassingly this was on the same date as the Port Talbot ceremony. I explained my dilemma to Peter Ashmore and he responded quite firmly: 'This is a situation where I believe Mother comes first!' Needless to say, Bob and Joan Scholey were immaculate hosts at Port Talbot. The ceremony went off perfectly and we were not missed.

Joyce and I were somewhat apprehensive about this visit to Windsor Castle, but during the welcoming party with the Royal Family we quickly felt relaxed and thoroughly enjoyed the whole congenial experience. The royals present were the Queen, the Duke of Edinburgh, the Queen Mother, The Princess Royal and Prince Edward. Among our fellow guests were the Nigel Lawsons, the Michael Heseltines, the David Attenboroughs and the Romanian ambassador and his wife.

In August I was approached by Peter Walker to succeed Ian MacGregor as Chairman of British Coal (the new name for the NCB), and this triggered off a discussion about who should be my successor at BSC in 1986. I had no reservations about telling Norman Tebbit that it would be a grave injustice if Bob Scholey did not succeed me. Whatever had happened in the last decade in improving BSC's fortunes, he had been the dominant architect and player. At times he displayed a 'Black Bob' image which was accepted and even admired within BSC but did not go down well with some ministers and civil servants. Norman, however, appreciated his robust style and we were at one in our thoughts about him as my successor. The Prime Minister, however, with the privatization of BSC clearly on the horizon, questioned whether my successor should not be from the private sector. Ronnie Halstead, then the Chairman of Beechams, was serving as a non-executive director of BSC and was making a commendable contribution. I suggested to Norman that Ronnie should be appointed the non-executive deputy chairman to support Bob, knowing that the Prime Minister had a high opinion of Ronnie. This plan fortunately proved acceptable to her.

It was planned that the succession should not be announced until later in the year. Unfortunately a board coup at Beechams in November led to Ronnie Halstead being ousted as their chairman. Brian Hayes, who had earlier succeeded Peter Carey as Permanent Secretary at the DTI, rang me, questioning whether it was still appropriate that Ronnie should become Deputy Chairman of BSC. Fortunately the Prime Minister was entertaining the members of the Nationalized Industries Chairmen's Group at Downing Street that very evening and, as Group Chairman, I was sitting next to her. The first thing she asked me was what I thought about the way Ronnie had been treated. I replied, 'Quite abominably.' She agreed with me and said: 'I will write to him tomorrow to express my condolences.' I then said: 'I do hope, Prime Minister, there is no question of a re-think about my succession?' To my relief she said: 'Leave it to me. I will ring Leon Brittan [who had recently replaced Norman Tebbit as Secretary of State] in the morning to ensure that does not happen!'

I enjoyed my few months working with Leon Brittan and later, during my British Coal days, he was very helpful to our cause in his role as a European Commissioner. In the last few weeks of my chairmanship Paul Channon took over as Secretary of State.

The announcement that Bob Scholey would succeed me was made in December, and never has an appointment been more justified. Another aspect of Bob, which few people appreciate, is that, contrary to his bluff image, he is a highly cultured man. I always found his knowledge of history and opera quite amazing. For many years I arranged a lunch in London for George and Mary Christie prior to the Glyndebourne season, and Bob Scholey was the only fellow guest who could match George's knowledge!

Returning to the restructuring of BSC, after the strike we rapidly accelerated our activities based on a plan agreed with the Government. The key features were:

(1)   BSC acquired the privately owned Aphasteel Ltd hot strip mill, which we then closed down. This raised BSC's production of strip mill products by some 10 per cent, under the quota allocations agreed with the European Union. Their continuous casting plant was transferred to Llanwern.

(2)   This made it possible to give an undertaking to maintain steel making at BSC's five major integrated sites, including Ravenscraig, for at least three years.

(3)   The closure of BSC's Gartcosh cold rolling mill, which was part of the Ravenscraig complex, was agreed. This was one of the most hotly contested closures we had experienced. During my period as Chairman of both BSC and Tate & Lyle I recorded the time spent accounting for what we were doing and also operating in a positive, creative role. In the case of BSC the former averaged at least 70 per cent – accounting to ministers, MPs, select committees, civil servants, trade union leaders, regional and local authorities, religious groups and other organizations. Immediately after the Gartcosh closure announcement this rose temporarily to over 90 per cent. This contrasted with an accountability factor of less than 20 per cent at Tate & Lyle. I soon came to the conclusion that one of my prime roles at BSC was to shield the executive directors as far as I could from this accountability load, so they could get on with the real job.

(4)   The Government agreed to support the establishment of the Phoenex II business with GKN. The new company – which combined the greater part of BSC's special steels business and the steel making and forging business of GKN – provided a formidable competitor in the European engineering steels market. This meant that virtually all BSC's ongoing business was focused on its primary steel making and any over-lap with the private sector was almost totally eliminated. In the previous six years, wholly owned assets of nearly £700 million had been divested in these mini-privatization deals.

(5)   BSC took a financial interest in Tuscaloosa Steel Corp. in the USA and supplied cast slabs from Teesside. Their new mill was of an advanced design and this venture was in line with BSC's policy of keeping abreast of best world practice.

Despite the adverse impact of the NUM strike, laudable progress was made in maintaining the momentum of restructuring BSC and in 1986 the corporation made a bottom-line profit of £38 million, the first since 1975, compared with a loss of £869 million in 1983 when I took over the chairmanship. The number of employees during the period 1983-6 was reduced from 81,000 to 54,000, reflecting a productivity improvement of about 32 per cent over the three years. We were also recognized as the best-performing steel business in Europe and our costs were lower than our US and European competitors. Only the Japanese were ahead of us. Overall we had well exceeded the objectives presented by Cecil Parkinson in 1983. Moreover, the prospect of privatizing BSC had become a reality.

Jake Stewart was Managing Director of the Strip Products Group and Gordon Sambrook of the General Steels Group. Gordon was also the architect of the Tuscaloosa deal. David Grieves led the personnel team, which had a heightened role during the NUM strike. Martin Llowarch was our managing director, finance, and I anticipated that he would probably become Bob Scholey's successor as Chairman, but he decided to move into the private sector. Brian Moffatt was the Works Director at Port Talbot; it was the only time in my experience that a man brought up essentially in the financial stream had taken on such a hands-on production role, made much more demanding by the impact of the strike and refurbishing the strip mill. He discharged his responsibilities with distinction, went on to succeed Bob as BSC Chairman and, not surprisingly, became Chairman of the Corus Group.

I was a member of the Nationalized Industries Group from 1983 to 1990 and became Chairman in 1985-6. It was a powerful group at that time, including such luminaries as Denis Rooke, Walter Marshall, Bob Reid, John King and Ron Dearing. Because I originated from the private sector and had been Personnel Director of ICI, I was always one of the two pushed forward to negotiate board members' salaries with ministers. My first involvement was in 1983, when we negotiated with Nigel Lawson and Norman Tebbit. They congratulated us on our presentation and agreed with most of it, but added that there was nothing they could do about it! It was clear to me from the outset that Margaret Thatcher felt people leading nationalized industries were performing a national service and their rewards should be accepted in that spirit. We continued this annual charade of negotiating with a team headed by the Chief Secretary to the Treasury, including John MacGregor and John Major. Although we made some modest improvements in relation to the remuneration of our equivalents in the private sector, there was still a glaring gap, which was to be fully demonstrated when nationalized industries were privatized.

One of my most vivid impressions at BSC was of the calibre of the board team, management and employees at all levels. In line with conventional views, I had not expected that they would match the quality I had known in the private sector, but gratifyingly this was proved wrong. Never were their qualities more clearly demonstrated than in the traumatic days of the NUM strike. I became increasingly depressed that their performance was not matched by their remuneration. I also pay a special tribute to the non-executive directors, Ronnie Halstead, John Gregson, John Boyd and Alan Wheatley, for their outstanding contributions during these challenging times. It was gratifying that many able people from the private sector were willing to serve in this way.

My normal days had consisted of mornings spent at British Steel and moving after lunch to Tate & Lyle, which seemed like a quiet oasis. But I was proud of the progress we made at both companies and there was no doubt that this was due to the exceptional performances of my two chief executives, Bob Scholey and Neil Shaw.

I then moved on full time to British Coal, where I knew I was to face the greatest challenge of my career.

9
British Coal: 1985–90

In August 1985, following the traumatic National Union of Mineworkers' strike, Peter Walker, the Secretary of State for Energy, asked me to call on him. Speaking on behalf of the Prime Minister and himself, he explained that they had become increasingly disenchanted with Ian MacGregor as the strike had progressed and did not want him to remain. I learned later that the desire to remove him stretched back to the time when he appeared stepping out of his car for a meeting with the NUM president, Arthur Scargill, and looking ridiculous with a paper bag over his head! They wished me to take over from MacGregor as Chairman of British Coal. Further, they believed such an announcement would cause him to depart. I replied that in normal circumstances I would be delighted to become Chairman, particularly as I would be rounding off my career in style, after leaving the industry as a young mining engineer thirty-eight years earlier. However, I knew his contract still had some twelve months to run, and I did not believe he would go before the end of it unless he was formally retired. Peter Walker explained that they did not feel able to do this, as it would be perceived as a victory for Scargill. Having served with MacGregor at British Steel for a few weeks, I explained that I would not be willing to serve with him in double harness at British Coal for potentially up to twelve months.

We eventually worked out a compromise solution, whereby I would join British Coal as MacGregor's announced successor, initially as a non-executive Deputy Chairman in November 1995, becoming fully executive in May 1996. As I predicted, MacGregor stayed to the end of his contract, having reluctantly accepted that I should gradually take over running the business, though he would obviously continue to chair the board meetings.

It was my second invitation to head up the coal industry. The first, at the time of Derek Ezra's impending retirement in 1982, was under very different circumstances. It came in a phone call when I was lying in a hospital bed, having suffered a brain haemorrhage. It happened in my later ICI days, when I would often fly by Concorde to America in the morning, have hectic meetings in New York, return on the night flight and go straight back to work at our Millbank headquarters. I will never forget sitting at home one evening after one such trip and suddenly experiencing an enormous blow on my head, like being coshed by a burglar. I called out to Joyce, who had gone up to bed, and she reacted calmly, in a typical English way by making a cup of tea. The headache continued to be intense so I phoned ICI's medical officer, who arranged for a doctor to call. He sent me immediately to Charing Cross Hospital. By then the pain had stopped and I felt a fraud, but they kept me in for a fortnight, doing tests, pumping in dyes and looking in my head for aneurysms, which fortunately I did not have. There was no operation though I was told to take things quietly for a while, play no golf for six months, not fly at night and to lose weight, which I did by dieting, shedding 3 of my bulky 18 stones.

The year 1985 had started on a good note when I became a Freeman of the City of London. But having accepted this second invitation to return to British Coal it was a difficult transition for MacGregor and for me. On joining British Coal, he made the major mistake of obviously mistrusting many people in top management, whom he had irritated by introducing a cabal of outside advisers. He also set up the Office of the Chief Executive, comprising himself and fellow Scot Jimmy Cowan. Along with the outside advisers, they formed an alternative management structure and took the decisions for the original management to carry out – a real recipe for confusion and conflict. There was also bitterness that respected figures – like Public Relations

Director Geoffrey Kirk, Industrial Relations Head Ned Smith, and Michael Eaton, the NCB's North Yorkshire Area Director, who was brought in as the board's principal public spokesman during the strike, following MacGregor's failure on television – had been summarily dispensed with because they could not go along with his approach and tactics. Management were later inflamed by MacGregor's book *The Enemies Within*, published as he was leaving the industry. They felt it should be classified as 'fiction'. Most of the management team mistrusted MacGregor and could not wait for him to go.

When I took over from him, I abandoned any residual involvement of his external advisers and also the Office of the Chief Executive. I was determined to re-establish the clear role of the original management team for whom, having seen them in action for a few months, I had formed a high opinion. I had not detected any weak links. Jimmy Cowan had by then retired and been replaced as Deputy Chairman by Kenneth Couzens, following a distinguished civil service career in the Treasury and also as Permanent Secretary at the Department of Energy. His insight and experience were invaluable to me and my colleagues. It was a classic example of a 'gamekeeper turned poacher', and his former colleagues had an unusual challenge to face, particularly in finding credible answers to the searching questions he was in the habit of asking. He also had an infectious sense of humour, something which was rather in short supply in those difficult days.

I had also considered whether I should have a chief executive, mirroring my rewarding relationship with Bob Scholey at British Steel. However, I became increasingly aware that John Northard, the Operations Director, was the key player in masterminding and carrying through the dramatic restructuring programme that was necessary and in 1988 he was promoted to be a Joint Deputy Chairman with Ken Couzens. This top structure served us well.

David Hunt was then serving as Peter Walker's number two and was very supportive of our efforts. He rather embarrassed me by spending more of his time underground than I did and in the process developed an admirable rapport with the miners.

To understand the evolving developments in the coal industry one had to look back to 1974, when the NUM were instrumental in bring-

ing down the Heath government. This left its mark in creating endur-
ing suspicions and tense relationships between the Conservative
leadership and the NUM.

Derek Ezra had taken over as Chairman of the NCB in 1971, having
served as a distinguished deputy chairman in the marketing field. In
1974 he negotiated the far-sighted Plan for Coal with the
Government, who agreed to contribute major investments to trans-
form operations and technology. This necessary though costly
blueprint to build a 'new' coal industry obviously had the full support
of the unions, hence it proceeded as a tripartite commitment. Ezra also
took justified pride in establishing a good relationship with Joe
Gormley, then the NUM president. But the increased productivity did
not come through in the 1970s as quickly as might have been
expected, in view of the vast capital investment. In 1981 Scargill
succeeded Gormley as President and Ezra realized that he had to accelerate the closure of uneconomic pits. However, the Government sadly
did not feel able to support his immediate closure programme, because
they believed there were inadequate coal stocks to risk a major strike
at that time.

In an eventful 14-month term as Chairman from July 1982, his
worthy successor Norman Siddall – a highly respected and forthright
mining engineer – again confronted the problem of closing uneconomic pits. He reminded the unions that the tripartite Plan for Coal
report envisaged taking out 3–4 million tonnes of coal mining capacity a year, though the outcome so far had been only 1 million tonnes.
The consequent burden on the industry created a major imbalance
between introducing new, low-cost capacity and pulling out of the old
high-cost pits. Looking at it another way, he said that 12 per cent of
the coal output lost £275 million in 1981/2 and this drain on the industry had to be remedied with as little hardship as possible for the people
involved. During Norman Siddall's chairmanship, sixteen mines were
closed, the manpower was reduced by 20,000 and productivity was
rising faster than for many years.

Announcing in the House of Commons MacGregor's appointment
as Chairman for three years from September 1983, Nigel Lawson, the
Secretary of State for Energy, set him clear objectives to continue the

task started by Siddall. These were to focus the industry's efforts on the earliest practicable return to profitability; to compete successfully in the marketplace and develop new markets for British Coal; and to secure the highest possible productivity and cost reductions.

The major problem facing the industry was the continuing burden of surplus high-cost coal being mined for about £6 a tonne more than customers were prepared to pay, and stocks piling up at the pitheads. Instead of facing up to this problem, militant union leaders had industrial action in mind and Scargill misled his members into an overtime ban in the autumn of 1983 and the year-long strike the following March. It was a bitter strike, attracting world media coverage and causing great hardship to many families after miners were inexcusably denied the opportunity by their union of a national ballot to decide their own destiny, because the militants knew the result would be negative. That was clear from the moderate coalfields, where every locally organized ballot fell short of the 55 per cent majority needed for strike action under union rules – most of them by a long way. It was far-sighted miners' leaders from these coalfields, where many miners stayed at work, who broke the NUM's long-standing monopoly by forming another union: the Union of Democratic Mineworkers.

I feel MacGregor's main mistake was believing that he could negotiate a solution with Scargill, as this could only be achieved by complete capitulation to all his extreme Marxist demands. During the later months of the strike, more disenchanted miners were gradually and encouragingly drifting back to work, and they and many of their families showed great courage in defying those still on strike. However, every time another fruitless negotiation was announced by Scargill and MacGregor, this flow was stopped or even reversed, in anticipation of a solution.

The strike ended after twelve months with no formal agreement on paper and Scargill beaten but still firmly in place as NUM president. He and his militant supporters were alone in regarding the strike as a success, mistakenly believing that their stance and tactics had been rewarded, despite the distressing sufferings of union members and their families.

Michael Eaton blamed the strike on antipathy between Scargill and

MacGregor, asking in a newspaper article, if Siddall could avoid a dispute, why could not his successor, given the remit of continuing the same policy? Eaton wrote:

> Negotiations came and went. There was no common ground. It became obvious that the only course left was a fight to the finish. Society suffered. Scargill repeated his rhetoric that no pit would ever close until totally exhausted. All this furore over a few mines which had no future anyway and which could have been closed in a civilized manner with very little hurt to anyone.

In his book, *The Actual Account*, Ned Smith, who was Head of Industrial Relations for most of the strike period, rejects the belief that the Government intended to 'take on' the NUM and reckons that, with greater management perseverance and the will to end it, the strike would have been over six months earlier.

Paul Routledge, in his book *Scargill – The Unauthorised Biography*, is in no doubt that the NUM left were determined to have a strike at the first opportunity. He comments: 'Cortonwood – a weak economic case, a moderate pit, an ambush by the Board – was not the perfect spring-board for the all-out conflict that Scargill undoubtedly wanted and which many of the men felt in their hearts was inevitable. But it was here and now and unavoidable.'

Peter Walker also comments on the origins of the strike in his book *Staying Power*.

> The ostensible cause of the start of the strike was the mishandling of Cortonwood pit. It was used by Arthur Scargill to call for immediate industrial action and backing from the other trade unions before a ballot took place. I personally believe the incident could have been handled better, both at local colliery and National Coal Board levels, but it was certainly not a justification for a nation-wide strike. Mr Scargill took advantage of an opportunity to create the strike.

What did trigger the strike? Having heard a great variety of views about how it occurred my own opinion is that, although the

Government had been expecting a showdown with Scargill at some point in the future, they did not perceive the Cortonwood closure as a reason for engineering a sudden major strike. It was nevertheless surprising that Scargill should use it at the time of high coal stocks combined with the imminent summer months of low coal demand. Clearly he must have realized and aimed to make it a long strike. The antipathy between him and MacGregor made this inevitable.

In my earlier industrial roles I had enjoyed very good relationships with union luminaries such as Hugh Scanlon, Len Murray, David Basnett, Clive Jenkins and Frank Chapple, and foolishly believed that there was a remote possibility of having a similar relationship with Scargill. However, this belief was very short-lived, and was dismissed at my first meeting with him and his executive colleagues at British Coal's Hobart House, London, headquarters immediately after I took up the chairmanship. He spent the first five minutes of his opening speech castigating my predecessor and, among other evils, claimed he was the ultimate confrontationalist – a fine example of 'a pot calling the kettle black'. He turned to me and said they had heard very good reports about me. He made a string of flattering remarks and said he was sure we would have a good working relationship. During this peroration, one of my colleagues passed a note along the table to me: 'Don't get carried away with this. He says this to every new chairman!' At midday I announced that we had a buffet lunch waiting upstairs, but Scargill immediately put his briefcase on the table and took out his sandwiches and vacuum flask. Everyone else came with us to the dining room except his confidant, the NUM secretary Peter Heathfield, who obviously felt someone had to stay with their boss.

What did surprise me was that the miners accepted me rather as 'one of the lads', presumably because I had worked underground for three years and had a Colliery Manager's Certificate. Despite the long gap since I had left the industry in 1947, I quickly established a rapport with most men during my underground visits. Though the highly mechanized underground mining processes were a revelation to me, I could still listen to deep discussions between my mining engineering colleagues and understand most of them.

There was a clause in the mineworkers' pension fund which said that strike service should count in calculating miners' pensions. We had contested this on the basis that a year's strike had never been contemplated but the NUM, not unexpectedly, challenged this view. The clash went right up the legal system and eventually the House of Lords found in our favour.

At our next meeting with Scargill and his team, he opened by saying this was a disgraceful outcome, that Margaret Thatcher had the judiciary in her pocket and there was no longer any justice in the UK. He then made the mistake of saying that not only should strike service count for pensions, but also breaks in service. I said: 'Arthur, that's the first point you have ever made with which I have some sympathy, because I happen to have thirty-eight years' broken service with British Coal.' Everyone in the room roared with laughter but not a flicker of a smile crossed his face. It was the only time I ever stopped him in full flow and he never returned to this subject again.

Scargill rang me one day and said he had a personal problem he would like to come and discuss, but he could not elaborate over the phone. I was a little wary about this, but arranged for my PA to join my secretary next door in case I might need him during the discussion. Scargill had recently been in the news about the purchase of a house in the Barnsley area for £125,000 and, considering that he had claimed not to have taken any salary during the strike, the media were asking how he could afford such a costly home. His response was that his daughter's boyfriend had bought the house and allowed him and his family to reside there. His immediate problem, as he outlined it to me, was that he could not sell his present house for the £40,000 asking price and he wondered if British Coal might buy it. I explained that, much as I would like to help, we were under the whip from the Government to sell as many of the 60,000 houses we currently owned and against that background I had to decline. It was a strangely friendly meeting and he accepted a cup of tea in the process, which in itself was a minor breakthrough in our relationship. It was also the first occasion he had been known to accept any hospitality within Hobart House.

Negotiating with Roy Lynk, the UDM president and his colleagues, could not have been more different from our dealings with the NUM.

The UDM took a more constructive and enlightened approach, compared with the continuing rigid adversarial stance of the other union. A classic example of this was the 1985/6 pay deal. An £8 a week rise was agreed with the UDM, but Scargill declined to discuss a pay deal for the NUM miners until many problems which flowed from the strike were resolved; for example, the treatment of residual pension issues and the future of dismissed miners. So we decided in the first few days of my chairmanship to apply the same pay deal arbitrarily to the NUM miners. This decision was somewhat influenced by the mood of the miners I had met during recent colliery visits, their constant theme being, 'Ignore Scargill – you are the gaffer. Get on with it.'

This initiative got banner headlines in the press. For example:

The Times – 'New coal chief snubs Scargill over wage deal'
The Guardian – 'For MacGregor the butcher read Haslam the mender of fences'
The Daily Mail – 'After the acerbic battle the canny consolidator'
The Northern Echo – 'The gaffer's good start'

This was some reputation to live up to!

During my chairmanship this negotiating process was repeated year after year and Scargill virtually abdicated his key role of negotiating wages and other working conditions. He continued to focus on negative militant issues and always seemed to be seeking reasons for the next strike or overtime ban, whereas after the strike we were determined to wipe the slate clean, in the hope that the NUM would share our views about the well-being of the industry and the aspirations of all our employees.

About this time I was infuriated by an article in the Sunday Telegraph by MacGregor's former adviser, David Hart, in which he claimed that British Coal managers regarded the UDM as a nuisance and were determined to weaken them. I replied quite categorically that I saw no validity whatsoever in his remarks. On the announcement of the new wage deal, UDM president Roy Lynk said it was a 'victory', whereas Scargill claimed it was 'diabolical'. That was their unmistakable answer to David Hart's scurrilous claim. In fact I greatly admired the role of Lynk and his UDM colleagues during the strike – both when they and their families suffered from flying pickets at their homes and at their mines and in our subsequent negotiations. Their positive though determined approach was in complete contrast to Scargill's negative rhetoric and it served the miners well. Any difficulties for our management in dealing with two unions were absolutely minimal compared with the advantages.

We continued to meet the NUM for discussions about the industry's problems and prospects and I was intrigued by the stance of the veteran Vice-President, Mick McGahey. When Scargill was in full flow making yet another rhetorical protest, McGahey would look at me shielding his face from Scargill's gaze – a sure signal that he had different views, as if to say, 'Don't believe this guy.' This gesture happened regularly and I thought how different our relationships would have been with McGahey as President instead of Scargill. That would undoubtedly have happened if Gormley had carried out his intention to retire early instead of soldiering on to sixty-five. This meant that McGahey, the favourite left-wing candidate for the post, could not stand for election having reached the age of 55 in 1980, which debarred him from the presidency under union rules. A left-winger and Chairman of the Communist Party, he was nevertheless respected by management as a man of integrity. He was basically concerned with the future well-being of the miners and their families and had none of the wider Marxist aspirations of Scargill such as bringing down the Government or reshaping society.

To avoid a potentially damaging strike in 1984 by the colliery officials union, NACODS, which would have brought all the mines to a standstill, including the UDM-manned pits, we had inherited from the Government a legal obligation to participate in a formal review procedure before we could close a pit judged to be uneconomic and with no future. Needless to say, Scargill opposed virtually every closure. These reviews, which were conducted rather like a court chaired by an umpire as an independent chairman, were extremely demanding on our management at all levels, but the roles played by John Northard and the Employee Relations Director, Kevan Hunt, were pivotal and highly commendable. The outcome was that every pit which we felt should be closed, we were able to carry through.

Most of the meetings with Scargill and the NUM executive focused on mine closures, with Scargill constantly questioning how many pits would be involved in the immediate future. We matched this by our reluctance to provide precise figures, as the forward market position was always deteriorating, with declining world coal prices making our financial targets even more difficult to achieve. Just announcing a total figure would only have caused rumour and speculation about which pits would be involved, whereas we were very willing to be frank and open in relation to any particular colliery becoming a potential closure candidate.

Much of our discussions focused on such items as flexible working, codes of working practice, the future of miners sacked in the strike and many residual pension problems. Gratifyingly we had virtually no strikes based on colliery closures. But we had to contend from time to time with overtime bans and rag-outs – brief strikes focused on an individual pit – and it is significant that 80 per cent of these occurred in the Yorkshire coalfield. These were obviously setbacks but not too damaging in the total picture. Gradually the miners themselves began to accept the economic facts of life and increasingly identified with the success of their pit and its future. Formally they felt they had to support Scargill in his role as NUM President, but in practice they became more and more reluctant to follow his militant demands and aspirations. For example, during overtime bans it was not unusual for some of the miners in the more enlightened coalfields to approach their colliery managers to see if they could work out a deal of superficially appearing to support the overtime ban without losing any coal production or wages.

When these set-piece discussions with the NUM executive took place, the media were always waiting outside to interview Scargill about the outcome. Our policy was then to invite the press and the television people into the office to hear our version which, needless to say, rarely matched Scargill's loaded pronouncements.

The outcome of all these discussions on closures led during my five-year term to the most rapid and extensive reconstruction in the UK's recent industrial history and I do not believe it has been matched before or since. The number of pits was reduced from 169 to 69 and our total manpower from 221,000 to 80,000 – a rather dramatic contrast, too, with the year-long strike which was caused by an announcement of the closure of six pits. These 100 closures were accomplished with only a small loss of deep-mine coal output, as we concentrated and expanded production at the lower-cost pits. The cost of producing coal was reduced by over 30 per cent and productivity was increased by nearly 100 per cent, equivalent to a rate of 14 per cent per annum.

Peter Walker was the first secretary of state of my chairmanship and I much appreciated his advice and support in those early days. There is no doubt in my mind that his strong role during the strike was a major factor in the successful outcome and his control of MacGregor avoided many potential catastrophes along the way. In his book *Staying Power* he says:

> The timing of the publication of Ian MacGregor's book was unfortunate for him and left a sour taste on the very day he left. He was coming in to say his goodbyes and I put the book on the table in front of where he was to sit, making it clear to him that I had read it. He sat uneasily in front of it. I said that I had read it and found it extraordinary that in the whole period we had worked together he had never made any criticism to my face. Now he had written a book in which he implied he was the wonder man and I had not got it right. If this was what he thought, he should have pointed out where he thought I was going wrong at the time.

This brought home to me the strong antipathy which existed between the two men. When I was working in double harness with MacGregor, on one occasion on our way to visit the Secretary of State, he said: 'I am absolutely fed up with the way he behaves and today I intend to tell him so to his face.' However, on arrival Walker immediately attacked MacGregor, whose head sank, with no response, and I had to vindicate his challenging criticism of British Coal's recent performances.

In the battle with the NUM leadership Peter Walker still retained a genuine sympathy with the miners themselves, and he was the architect of the very generous redundancy terms which the Government allowed us to use. Without these we could not have achieved this rapid and deep restructuring. Every miner was offered either redundancy terms or a transfer to a low-cost pit in his locality, so there were no enforced redundancies. Redundancy terms were particularly generous for miners over fifty, who were pensionable, and by 1990 this was reflected in the average age of the underground workers having fallen to an all-time low of thirty-five years.

Initially I did not relish the media activity which surrounded my chairmanship of British Coal, but it was impossible to avoid. With Scargill always being in the news I felt it was essential to make myself available to the media as much as I could. TV was specially demanding, particularly in studio discussions with such luminaries as Jeremy Paxman and Peter Snow, who always hoped to front a discussion with Scargill and myself. I was always willing but it never happened.

Two interviewers I particularly welcomed were ITN's industrial correspondent Ian Ross and IRN's Geoffrey Goodman. Not that they gave me an easy time – far from it! But we always had a helpful pre-interview chat. In all my dealings with interviewers and journalists over the years I have never been let down by publication of an off-the-record comment, though some business friends I meet nowadays are obviously not so fortunate.

Conversely, I was much more at ease when emerging from an underground pit visit, when it was not unusual to find a local TV unit waiting to interview me. On one amusing occasion a young woman interviewer broadened the questions to British Coal's wider issues and in response I referred to the fact that one of our problems was that we had too many hard faces. She immediately asked me to name the colleagues with the hardest faces! I put my hand over the camera lens and gave her a brief tutorial on the subject of the tough mining conditions encountered on too many of our coal faces!

Newspapers right across the spectrum were generally supportive and helpful, but an exceptional contribution came regularly from an unlikely source – Woodrow Wyatt writing in the *News of the World*, and there is no doubt his articles had a real impact, particularly on miners' wives. One Sunday, commenting on yet another NUM overtime ban, he wrote:

One day miners will understand that Scargill is not interested in their welfare. His Marxist obsession is with overthrowing the Government by halting industry. Last week *The Times* foolishly criticized Sir Robert Haslam, Chairman of British Coal. It said his communications were bad. Nonsense, the bright tabloid *Coal News* is delivered to all miners' homes. It tells them all the facts about coal. It is not Sir Robert's fault that many miners prefer to swallow Scargill's lies.

Incidentally, *Coal News* won top awards for company tabloid newspapers.

This caused further comment in his book *The Journals of Woodrow Wyatt*, in volume I of which he described a discussion with the Prime Minister.

> We discussed Haslam; I said, 'He is a very good fellow,' with which she agreed. I said, 'I'm glad you think so. *The Times* were very silly in attacking him.'

Margaret Thatcher felt it was due to David Hart who was so keen on supporting the Union of Democratic Mineworkers that he failed to understand the difficulties British Coal faced in being fair and even-handed.

British Coal had many related organizations and never in my life I had I received so many requests to make speeches. In my early days, before I learned to pace myself, I once made five speeches in seven evenings, including the weekend. I was embarrassed to find that one of the audience was visibly there on all five occasions. While coolly complimenting me each evening, he was very critical of the fact that I was changing the statistics from night to night!

Another unusual feature of my job was that Joyce and I were regularly invited to charity functions, with the intention that I would be auctioned to take a winning couple on an underground visit. To my amazement people were bidding £3,000 and more for this dubious privilege! Surprisingly the men who had done the bidding rarely came and I was usually entertaining two ladies or a wife and son. The miners on the face clearly welcomed these visitors and joined in the spirit of the occasion.

I was proud of the achievements of British Coal (Enterprise), which was introduced following the success of its sister organization in British Steel. In those five years 50,000 new job opportunities were created in mining communities with BCE's assistance and over 10,000 redundant miners were found alternative employment through our Job Shop Scheme. Again, this could not have been achieved without the sympathetic and generous support of the Conservative government.

Over the five-year period our opencast coal activities increased from 14 million to 17 million tonnes per annum. Our relationships with the mining contractor companies who worked the sites on our behalf were harmonious and mutually beneficial. Clearly while the sites were being worked they were a blight to the local communities, but our land restoration policies were, I believe, highly regarded. While the restoration of sites to agricultural land was the most common, more and more schemes created wildlife and nature reserves, leisure parks, cricket grounds, golf courses and many other local amenities. Ray Proctor, who was Managing Director of British Coal Opencast, did a splendid balancing act, providing low-cost coal and negotiating with local communities to improve amenities.

On the marketing front, British Coal was selling about 80 per cent of its output to power stations, which then generated nearly two-thirds of the nation's electricity – coal by wire we called it. Initially the CEGB was our prime customer but, following privatization of the electricity industry, we were dealing with the demerged National Power and PowerGen, with whom we signed three-year contracts in April 1990.

Malcolm Edwards was our knowledgeable commercial and marketing director. He was highly regarded in both the European and Commonwealth coal industries as a prime authority on the marketing aspects of our industry and his views were widely sought. He also brought an extra discipline to our board deliberations when we discussed closing potential uneconomic pits, by stressing that the quality of the coal being produced should also influence our decisions. Humorously, Malcolm would declare that a long-standing customer he knew had been buying coal from a particular seam for many years and to cut it off would be a catastrophe. Alas we often could not continue to oblige but he had the knack of conjuring replacement supplies from elsewhere to keep the customer happy. We were lucky to have him and his obvious talents in this marketing role.

Throughout this period we were under intensely fierce pressure either from natural gas or imported coal from the USA, Australia and South Africa. Some commentators expressed the view that our mines could not be very efficient. They failed to realize that we have been mining coal in this country for 500 years. The best reserves have been worked out and all the remaining coal is at a great depth and the seams are relatively thin. I believe that no country in the world, mining coal in the same conditions as ourselves, could match our costs. Germany was subsidizing its coal mines to the extent of £4 billion per annum, with the result that we were closing UK pits which had much lower costs than even the best in Germany. So virtually no imports were finding their way into Germany or Spain – another protected industry – and we were absorbing nearly all the international coal available. This situation was further compounded when our government signed a long-term contract with EdF, the nationalized electricity industry in France, to supply highly subsidized nuclear energy to the UK through the Channel Link which was equivalent to the output of eight large coal mines. Ironically, the link had been fathered by Tony Benn, then at the Board of Trade, to export cheap electricity produced from UK coal to France!

I made frequent visits to the European Commission in Brussels for discussions with Commissioners and their colleagues, where I voiced my concerns about the anti-competitive regimes existing in Germany, France and Spain, and also about import of dumped coal from Russia, Poland and China. Although the discussions were often encouraging, follow-up action was sadly lacking, possibly because our government were not seen to be solidly supportive. We also discussed the development of clean coal technology and Brussels did support financially our experimental programme at Yorkshire's Grimethorpe Colliery. Alas, we had to abandon it eventually for lack of future resources. It is ironical that twelve years later, clean coal technology has emerged as an exciting new concept!

In 1987 Cecil Parkinson took over from Peter Walker as Secretary

Bolton School captain in his teens, Bob Haslam often returned as president of the Old Boltonians' Association and, for seven years from 1990, as chairman of the governors – ensuring there were always laughs at the yearly prizegivings

Princess Diana opened Bolton School's new arts centre in 1993. Just before leaving, two sixth formers abseiled down the central tower and presented her with the legendary box of chocolates

In the crypt of the Palace of Westminster, Lord Haslam married Elizabeth Sieff, his second wife, in 1996

A bronze bust was commissioned to mark retirement in 1990 after five years as council chairman of Manchester Business School

Created a life peer in 1990, he chose the title The Lord Haslam of Bolton. Bolton was the Lancashire town of his early formative years where he lived with his family and was captain of local schools

Introducing Virginia Bottomley (*right*, with Lady Elizabeth Haslam) at the tenth anniversary in 1996 of the children's welfare national charity, The Michael Sieff Foundation, Lord Haslam recalled he and their chief guest were long-standing friends, having first met her on a family outing when he was left holding her as a weeping baby!

Fund raising for The Police Rehabilitation Trust – Lord and Lady Haslam at the Prince of Wales' reception in May 2002

Well and truly Haslamed!
Paints Division 1975-1979

Bob Haslam always enjoyed a laugh during his time as a captain of British industry. Being 'Haslamed' in ICI meant the welcome experience of getting a salary grade – in an industry-wide structure for all posts up to middle managers devised by the Haslam Panel during an intensive eighteen-month study

When chairman of Tate & Lyle – where the Mr Cube cartoon character had been widely used – Bob Haslam joined British Steel (in 1983) to become chairman and restructure the industry. He praised the steel trade union leader for his courageous leadership during the coal strike – though Bill Sirs looks apprehensive in this Ron McTrusty cartoon

Bob Haslam as Mrs Mop. Ron McTrusty's cartoon has energy secretary of state Peter Walker inviting the British Steel chairman in 1985 to move to coal and 'tidy up' the industry after Ian MacGregor's controversial reign

Having first worked underground in the coal industry thirty-eight years before, Bob Haslam returns in 1985 as 'one of t'lads' – to become chairman. Mining union leader Arthur Scargill, looking worried in the background of this Richard Willson cartoon, continued to focus on militant negative issues . . . and virtually abdicated his key role of negotiating wages and other working conditions of State for Energy and we immediately resumed the warm and positive working relationship we had earlier at British Steel. His thoughts on the business aspects of the coal industry were spot on, and equally he had a valuable input on some of the industrial relations problems we were facing with both the NUM and NACODS. Sometimes we spoke on Sunday evenings about a potential strike or overtime ban and when occasionally we had a different view he was usually proved right. His long-term objective was that British Coal should be privatized and he announced this at the 1988 Conservative Party conference. Needless to say I shared this ambition, but this led us into discussions about the need for a revision in the way British Coal's financial results were presented.

In 1988 Cecil and I had an exploratory discussion about whether I would sign another three-year contract and I expressed my initial reluctance. Cecil responded, 'John King, who is older than you, has just signed another contract with British Airways.' I replied: 'You get John to come and run British Coal for three years and I will happily sign a double contract at British Airways!' We finally compromised and I signed to remain as Chairman until the end of 1990.

The financial support provided by the Government to British Coal over the years was not by cash injections but as loans. Throughout my term our results were bedevilled by the incredibly high interest charges paid to the Government on these massive loans. In 1990 these charges, which in a private-sector company would have been regarded as dividends, amounted to £574 million. Exceptional restructuring costs and writing off redundant assets amounted to another £472 million. The Government agreed that this was unacceptable and in March 1990 the desired changes were introduced by John Wakeham, who took over from Cecil Parkinson in 1989. British Coal's finances were reconstructed by writing off our debts and making provision for historical liabilities. As a result, the 1990 accounts reflected the real performance of the current business, with an operating profit of £238 million and, for the first time for many years, a bottom-line profit of £78 million – modest, but a step in the right direction. Privatizing the coal industry became a realistic possibility.

John Wakeham, too, was helpful and supportive. His wife had been killed in the ghastly Brighton bomb incident, and he had suffered serious leg injuries. Soon after becoming our secretary of state he courageously said that he would like to make a pit visit. Going underground and travelling a coal face is a daunting experience for a visitor even one who is fighting fit. But John Wakeham, even with his obvious infirmity, took it in his stride and miners at the North-east's Westoe colliery really warmed to him for making the commendable effort.

The year 1989 was the centenary of the Institution of Mining Engineers and I was asked to be President during this historic year, having earlier become a Companion of the Institution of Mining Electrical and Mining Mechanical Engineers. The centenary involved a wide range of celebrations, including a dinner at the Guildhall, a service of thanksgiving at York Minster, and the culminating event at the Banqueting House, London, in January 1990, which was attended by a distinguished array of people directly or indirectly involved in the coal industry.

John Wakeham was the chief guest, and reiterated that the recent capital reconstruction 'will provide coal with its best opportunity for years to compete on an equal footing at the start of the 1990s unencumbered by the financial burdens of the past'. But he warned that for all the remarkable recent progress that had been made in the UK coal industry, the Institution of Mining Engineers was still faced with 'a series of challenges which have combined to put the members of this Institution on the front line of perhaps the greatest challenge in the industry since nationalization forty-odd years ago'. This prophetic view was certainly proved correct.

Michael Butler was our able and unflappable finance director, whose advice and support I greatly appreciated in these critical discussions with government. At that time our pension funds amounted in value to some £19 billion – then one of the biggest company funds in the UK – and Michael's role was impressive. Commentators often gave the impression that the financial fraternity in the nationalized industries were really amateurish. I have several company pensions – ICI, Tate & Lyle, and British Steel/British Coal – and the performance of the British Coal funds has excelled them all, despite the fact that investment policy and decisions in those days were all taken in-house, whereas the others were relying on City advisers. They were also the creators of the successful CINVEN organization, formerly the capital venture arm of the pension funds and now one of Europe's leading private equity providers. We were fortunate to have Hugh Jenkins and then David Prosser heading our funds, though understandably they were persuaded to move on to top jobs in the insurance world with salaries and opportunities we could not match.

My relations with junior ministers, leading Opposition spokesmen and MPs were a source of many interesting contrasts. Some junior ministers and MPs would summon me to the House of Commons if there was a pit in their constituency under threat of closure. In sharp contrast Ken Clarke, when he was Secretary of State for Health, would phone me in his capacity as MP and ask if could he come and see me about a problem in one of his constituency pits. Neil Kinnock, the Leader of the Opposition, would also ring me to ask if he could come for breakfast at Hobart House to discuss his pits at Ebbw Vale. He had an incredible knowledge of what was happening, even about the state of individual coal faces, so I had to ask our South Wales Area Director to join us and deal with his pertinent and detailed points. It was at this time I first met Tony Blair, then an opposition front bench spokesman. We had a deep discussion on energy and employment issues and I immediately formed a high opinion of his personal qualities, an opinion which I hold to this day, despite my Conservative allegiance.

My highlights, of course, were when, from time to time, I was summoned to have discussions with the Prime Minister at Number 10, sometimes on my own, sometimes with the Secretary of State present. The main topic was usually that we were not doing enough for the UDM. The second was usually what Scargill was plotting and whether there was any possibility of him getting out of his box again. I tried to reassure her on both issues and in the process was always impressed by her knowledge of what was happening in the coalfields. I welcomed these audiences but our exchanges were robust and challenging. I always felt I had a fair hearing, however, although with her normal parting shot of 'You must do even more for the UDM' still ringing in my ears!

131

Away from the mainstream activities of British Coal there were many enjoyable experiences. A special highlight was the official launch of the new Selby mining complex in Yorkshire in December 1989, when the Queen and the Duke of Edinburgh had graciously agreed to be present to perform the opening ceremony. The day before, we took Sir William Heseltine, the Queen's private secretary, and Sir Marcus Worsley, then the High Sheriff, on a dummy run to the Riccall Colliery coal face, which the Royal Party would visit while underground. The plan had been to take the Queen and others about 40 yards along the coal face and then all retreat back to the main roadway. The High Sheriff said he was not happy about this, as the Queen always had to lead. I explained that, in the very cramped conditions, it would be difficult for her to do this without embracing each member of the retinue *en route*, and that the only alternative would be for her to lead us all the way along the 240-yard long face, which would be very demanding. This problem was left for further discussion when we returned to the surface.

This problem did not need to be resolved, for a disappointing reason: we were informed that the Queen had flu and would not be able to come, but that fortunately the Duke of Edinburgh would still be with us. The underground visit went extremely well, and the Duke seemed to thoroughly enjoy his rapport with the miners and they responded warmly. His whole demeanour that day was immaculate and went a long way to make up for the disappointment of the Queen's absence.

When we were coming up the pit shaft in the cage, the Duke asked me about his role at the lunch we were to have with representatives of the wide range of parties who had contributed to the success of the project. I said we were hoping he would unveil a plaque to mark the opening. He looked at me, rather puzzled, and incredulously repeated, 'Unveil a plaque?' In the middle of the night Albert Tuke, the North Yorkshire Area Director, had the ceremonial bronze plaque modified so that 'Presence of the Queen' had been taken out and the Duke of Edinburgh's role highlighted. When he pulled the string to unveil the plaque, he again looked extremely surprised, but then laughed and said: 'Thank God it wasn't carved out in stone!' It was a memorable day for everyone who had been involved with the project, and we were highly indebted to the Duke for his outstanding contribution.

In 1988, we were asked by the hard coal industry in Poland to advise them on how to restructure in the way we had transformed our own. They also made a similar approach to Ruhrkohle in Germany, but after consultations they decided to award us the contract. This involved me and Ken Moses, our technical director, making visits to Warsaw and Katowice. Ken quickly took over the focal role of this consultancy and did a remarkable job, which clearly impressed the Polish mining engineers.

The geological problems and the mining equipment in the Polish mines were similar to our own and the people then running the industry were obviously highly capable mining engineers. But the mines, and particularly the support and ancillary services, were greatly overmanned, so they were starting from an even more difficult base than British Coal. On the first visit Ken and I addressed the leaders of their research and development activities at Katowice. It was almost like a university campus, with as many as 3,000 people involved, compared with 450 at our equivalent unit at Bretby in the Midlands. On a visit to their largest colliery we could not go underground because the miners were on strike that day, so we were taken on a tour of the surface facilities. From our discussions, it was clear that they ran the mine effectively, but the many ancillary facilities were mind-boggling – for example, they had a health centre for the miners and a forty-bed hospital on the site. On returning to the colliery offices, which were about three times larger than our biggest pit office, we had to walk through a group of 1,000 striking miners. I was a little apprehensive, but the Manager said, 'No need to worry, they were just admiring your embassy man's Jaguar and wondering if they would ever own one.'

Our next visit followed the change of government after the collapse of Communism. Amazingly the people we had been dealing with had been completely replaced and we were now involved with economists and academics rather than mining engineers. We also visited one major pit being run by a well-meaning Solidarity supporter who was only twenty-six years old and clearly did not know the first thing about mining.

I was privileged to meet Lech Walesa three times when he was Chairman of Solidarity and subsequently when he became President of the republic. The first time was at a lunch chaired by our Foreign Secretary, Douglas Hurd, and then at a Bank of England lunch. On both occasions we had brief discussions about my views on the future of their coal industry, and I explained what a formidable restructuring task they faced. He expressed appreciation of the help and advice we were giving. However, our recommendations could only be followed to a limited degree, because it was obvious the manpower reduction needed was monumental, and there was no way this could be achieved on the voluntary redundancy basis linked to generous severance terms which had made possible our own restructuring.

Our third meeting was at the Polish embassy, when their ambassador had invited UK business leaders to meet Lech Walesa. However, he had also invited Miss Poland, who I believe had just won the Miss World title. She was sitting comfortably next to her President, and it was very obvious that he was much more interested in her than the rest of us!

I had occasional contacts with Robert Maxwell, usually on the telephone. These normally involved him offering some 'unbelievable investment opportunities' for our substantial pension funds, which seemed to have an aphrodisiac effect on him. I really could not understand why so many of our business leaders were willing to support him and even fawned on him, and I consistently resisted his blandishments. About 7.30 one Sunday morning my phone rang. It was Maxwell's secretary explaining that her boss needed to speak to me urgently. Although I was in bed, I got the impression I was expected to spring to attention. After a long pause he came on and said: 'Bob I badly need your help.' He explained that we and the British Rail pension funds owned a piece of land which he wished to acquire for his *Daily Mirror* delivery vans. Irritably I replied that I had no idea what he was talking about and had no intention of finding out, but that I would give him the name of a young man in our pension fund who might be able to help. Fortunately he put the phone down on me and gratifyingly it was our last contact!

Another unusual experience started with a phone call from Norris

McWhirter, who asked whether I knew that, according to his *Guinness Book of Records*, one of our South Wales mining pensioners was now the oldest man in Europe, and in the next few days would have his 112th birthday. He suggested that it would be great to give him a joint lunch in London. I doubted if he would be capable of travelling from the South Wales valleys but said I would get my colleagues to check. The pensioner, John Evans, surprised us all by saying he had never been to London and would be delighted to come!

We arranged train travel and he arrived with his son, Amwel, aged eighty-four, whom he embarrassingly treated like a schoolboy. At lunch John was obviously not interested in food and as each course came he pushed his and my plates away and continued to draw on the table cloth, explaining to me how we had worked his pit in the wrong way. Remarkably, he had worked underground, mainly at the coal face, for sixty-two years, retiring at the age of seventy-five in 1952, when his pit was closed. From time to time his son was summoned to provide a pen or support his father's arguments and, despite my protests, he spent most of the meal standing at his father's elbow. The other surprising feature was that, with his agreement, I subsequently arranged for his lungs to be X-rayed, and there was no evidence of any dust contamination. As we parted I said we would like to give him a birthday present and he asked for one of those Walkman gadgets he had heard about, so that he could play his beloved music while strolling around his garden. He was a really great survivor, and a privilege to meet. Sadly he died six months later.

In the last few months of my chairmanship we had a series of presentations and discussions with John Wakeham and his senior civil servants about the long-term size and shape of the coal industry. We argued that it should be based ideally on forty low-cost pits combined with the widescale use of clean coal technology in electricity generation to contain any carbon dioxide emission problems. A prime reason was that it would allow access to all the workable remaining coal reserves in the UK without the prohibitively high cost of sinking new shafts and building new surface plants. Sadly this minimum level of pits was breached in a monumental way in 1993, as I will describe in Chapter 13.

After my departure early in 1991 my former colleagues, under the chairmanship of my successor, Neil Clarke, continued the process of restructuring the industry and sharply improving productivity and costs. By October 1992 the number of pits had been reduced to fifty. Against this background I was astonished to hear on television news on 13 October that Michael Heseltine had announced the closure of a further thirty-one pits, with the loss of 31,000 jobs. I understand that Neil Clarke and British Coal went along with this announcement, though reluctantly. I could not recollect a government minister making such an announcement before and if I had still been Chairman and could not have prevented it, I would have regarded it as a resigning matter. We always avoided making dramatic statements like that as they are bound to be highly disruptive and unproductive.

Moreover it was a staggering political blunder to announce devastating cuts in the depth of a biting recession, when all the experience of recent years showed that the industry was capable of facing up to market forces in a measured way. There was an understandable outcry, also unexpectedly from 'Middle England' and rebel Tory backbenchers. Arthur Scargill leaped out of his box, this time with some cause, using his familiar rhetoric by condemning 'the most savage, brutal act of vandalism in modern times'. For the first time he was gaining popular public support and unusual allies.

Paul Routledge, in his book on Scargill, comments on the massive march of miners and their families through London's West End.

> It was the biggest outpouring of public wrath since the poll tax demonstrations, but it was peaceful . . . Guests in the posh hotels of Kensington and Knightsbridge leaned out of their windows and cheered. Shoppers and tourists clapped, motorists tooted their horns . . . when the march passed the five-star Royal Garden Hotel, a miner gesticulated to cheering guests: 'Look, they're rattling their jewellery for Arthur.'

Routledge concludes: 'Heseltine had achieved the impossible. He had put "our Arthur" back on his pedestal.'

John Major, in his autobiography, reports on the storm raging after the announcement: 'I chaired a European summit in Birmingham. It was too good an opportunity for the miners to miss. They took to the streets to demonstrate against pit closures and their chanting of "Coal for ever!" drifted up to us. Blissfully unaware of the background, Helmut Kohl [then the German Chancellor] beamed happily and waved back to them.' This was not surprising, as he was probably reflecting on the virtues of the measured way he was supporting his own coal industry.

John Major also describes the announcement as 'a mistake that was to inflame public opinion more spontaneously than any other event in my years in Downing Street.' He continues: 'The prospect of whole mining communities being destroyed touched a raw nerve among the British people – including grassroots Conservatives, who understandably felt we had a moral obligation especially to the Nottinghamshire miners in the UDM who had continued working throughout the long coal strike . . .'

Bowing to the storm of national protests, Heseltine announced a U-turn six days later. The High Court decided in December that the Government and British Coal had acted 'unlawfully and irrationally' by ignoring the rights of mineworkers and unions to be consulted over pit closures. The row rumbled on as the Government appointed consultants to report on the viability of the mines earmarked for closure. It did not begin to subside until five months after the fatal announcement. The Coal White Paper unveiled plans to reprieve twelve of the thirty-one threatened pits, provided hope of rescue for another seven pits, and offer the other twelve, which British Coal intended to stop mining, to the private sector. Full privatization was promised in the next parliamentary session.

An interesting sequel occurred when Heseltine met the Energy Group in the House of Lords. He argued that the announcement was a response to the lack of progress by British Coal in improving productivity. I questioned him, on the basis of 100 per cent productivity improvements during my chairmanship, representing an annual increase of 14 per cent, and I asked whether he could name any other British industrial company in recent times which could match that. He did not respond.

I was always convinced the coal industry should have been privatized before the electricity industry, as my former business was always likely to be a very difficult privatization. Nevertheless, it was fortunately though reluctantly accepted that the core of the industry should be sold off as a single unit. With high hopes that RTZ might buy it, I had some exploratory discussions with Derek Birkin and Bob Wilson, then Chairman and Chief Executive, but their board eventually turned it down because, I believe, a number of the non-executive directors were opposed. This was sad as there is no doubt that, with their enviable mining experience and clout, they could have made a much better job of it than RJB Mining, the eventual successful bidder.

Another issue which arose during the closing period of my chairmanship was the question of my successor. David Kendall, who had had a successful career with BP, joined us in 1989 as Deputy Chairman and as a potential successor. He settled in very well and was quickly able to make an effective contribution. However, he seemed to decide that British Coal was not for him and went off to become Chairman of Bunzl in 1990, followed by a series of other private-sector chairmanships for which he had been in obvious demand.

My logical successor seemed to me to be either John Northard or John Parker, then a part-time board member. I realized, however, that in the run-up to privatization, the Government would prefer a chairman from the private sector. I had got to know John Parker well during my British Steel days, when he was Chairman of Harland & Wolff, and was extremely impressed with his performance in this daunting role when the troubles in Northern Ireland were at their highest point. I invited him to join the British Coal board and was delighted when he accepted. He made a fine contribution to our deliberations, but became something of an embarrassment to me, as he appeared to be making more underground pit visits than I was! He had an immediate rapport with the miners and was equally admired by the management. It was clear that he would have been widely welcomed as my successor. However, the civil servants had dug up an auditor's report on Harland & Wolff, which cast doubts on his financial abilities. Well, you could have fooled me – he went on to become Chairman of Babcock International, where he did a fine job in restoring their fortunes.

Recently he became Chairman of Lattice – now National Grid Transco – and I understand he would have been the preferred choice as the new chairman of Railtrack but had to decline because of his wife's indisposition.

The search for my successor was protracted and it was only a few days before Christmas that John Wakeham told me they had appointed Neil Clarke and hoped I would be happy with the choice. I had never met Neil so could not proffer any view, but my belief that John Parker would have been a far better chairman was soon confirmed.

My years at British Coal were the most challenging of my career. Rapidly retrenching a major industry in a shrinking market is an infinitely more difficult management task than developing a business in an expanding market. You really do have to be able to play all the keys on the piano.

It would be remiss to close this chapter without emphasizing the great contribution made by the board members. We were extremely well served by our part-time members, David Atterton, Colin Barker, Ron Dearing, David Donne, Johan Erbé, David Newbigging, John Parker, Melvyn Rosser and David Walker, who collectively brought great experience and wisdom to our deliberations at critical times.

I have already referred to the sterling qualities of my executive board colleagues. As a team they could not have been excelled in the balanced way they analysed and determined the best solution to so many problems. I owe all the executive and part-time directors a great debt for their support and forbearance.

The area directors and their senior colleagues in the coalfields and the colliery managers and their teams had the daunting task of implementing the closure programme – carried out in a continuing adversarial ambience sustained by the militant elements of the NUM. They were key players in the successful implementation of our retrenchment activities.

It is somewhat invidious to comment on the roles of individual head office departments, as they were all worthy contributors, but two deserve a special mention, namely the industrial relations and the public relations teams as they, too, were both at the heart of our retrenchment activities.

The IR team were led by Kevan Hunt, who was one of the best industrial relations managers I have ever worked with. He and his colleagues coped incredibly well with the legion of problems posed by the activities of Scargill and his militant followers. They also now had to deal with two miners' unions, the NUM and the UDM, and this frequently led to criticism of not being even-handed. But from my perspective they did a commendable job in maintaining a fair balance.

The PR team was led by Norman Woodhouse, again a very competent and able operator. He quietly encouraged me to participate in the news conferences and interviews requested by national and regional journalists. Hence, we had regular informal briefing meetings – by popular request usually over lunch – with editors and columnists interested in our problems and prospects. More importantly our PR team, both in London and in the coalfields, had a good rapport with journalists and were adept at getting across positive stories and fending off misguided criticism. Our internal communications, I believe, compared well with the best in British industry.

As in British Steel, I was extremely fortunate to have such high-calibre board colleagues and senior managers, who were just as capable as their opposite numbers in comparable private-sector companies and yet surprisingly they never complained about their much lower remuneration for their sterling efforts. Few managements have faced a more gruelling challenge, and on reflection I doubt whether any other team could have matched their performance. What has been even more sad is that, following privatization, virtually none of the senior members of British Coal benefited from the higher salaries, stock options and all the other trappings of the private sector. This was in sharp contrast to their opposite numbers in other comparable industries privatized during that period.

Finally, reflecting on my period at British Coal, it was rewarding and at times enjoyable but with some strong masochistic undertones! Even so, I was extremely lucky to have this opportunity and it will always remain the pinnacle of my career.

10
Semi-retirement

As my retirement date from British Coal drew near, I had approaches from various companies offering me a variety of roles, but two stood out. The first was from a close friend, Gordon Booth, on behalf of Bechtel Group to become Chairman of Bechtel Ltd. The other was from Bruce Wasserstein, who reminded me of my debt to them for the unpaid help and support he and Jeffrey Rosen had given us during my ICI sojourn in the USA. He explained that Wasserstein Perella & Co were planning to establish a London office to manage their affairs in the UK and Europe and would like me to chair this new operation. I accepted both these part-time chairman offers with enthusiasm.

Bechtel Ltd: 1991–4
Bechtel is a remarkable global company which celebrated its centenary in 1998 and unbelievably had only four family chairmen during this period. Reflecting on the accepted concept that family-run businesses usually run out of steam, Bechtel must be the outstanding exception. As little is generally known about this fascinating business, I will briefly review some of the earlier highlights.

In 1898 a Kansas rancher, Warren A. Bechtel, became disillusioned with farming and decided to carve out a career in construction. The scale of his operations rapidly increased and in the 1920s his efforts were focused on railroad, highway and pipeline construction jobs in California and Oregon. Stationed in a plaza at Bechtel's headquarters is a replica of an old railroad coach, emblazoned with 'W.A. Bechtel & Company' and in smaller letters, the name 'WaaTeeKaa'. The original was the home of Warren's son, Stephen D. Bechtel, Snr, and his family. It highlighted that getting as close as possible to the work site has always been a Bechtel hallmark. But bigger things were in store and in 1931 a Bechtel consortium secured the contract to build the Hoover Dam, the biggest civil engineering project ever undertaken at that time. Sadly, W.A. did not live to see this historic work completed, as he died suddenly on a visit to Moscow in August 1933 and was succeeded by his son, Steve. The dam was completed more than two years ahead of schedule and in September 1935 President Roosevelt officially dedicated the dam saying: 'I came, I saw and I was conquered, as everyone will be who sees for the first time this great feat of mankind.' The Hoover Dam was a pivotal event in the history of Bechtel.

Steve Bechtel brought a new dimension to the business because of his interest in pipelines, along with closely associated developments in petroleum and its by-products. Bechtel built its first refinery in 1937 and by late 1941 had eleven refineries completed or under way. With Steve's thoughts focused on petroleum, it would only be a matter of time before he began looking at the Middle East.

Steve had been pushing hard to move Bechtel beyond the United States and in 1940 he succeeded with the construction of a 50-mile oil pipeline in Venezuela, including 40 miles of road plus a harbour and wharf installation. He had the daunting task of leading the company through the war years, and separately became heavily involved in ship-building. Bechtel people were drawn into some hair-raising adventures in the Pacific. They built the top-secret Canol project – a 1,430-mile pipeline spanning portions of Alaska, the Yukon and the North-west Territories. The Bechtel joint venture had to make the region habitable by building roads, airstrips, housing and communication centres, starting from a base camp north of Edmonton, Alberta.

During the two years of construction Steve became a sub-Arctic commuter, staying in touch with the field crews. Eventually the heavy demand of travelling to the Arctic, the Pacific and the Middle East and the never-ending need to stay on top of dozens of projects, took their toll. By the time peace was declared in 1945, he was physically exhausted.

He took a short respite, as Bechtel Brothers McCone Co. was formed in place of two other Bechtel companies. By 1946 he had had enough of retirement and took the reins as President of the new firm. The following year he headed off on his first post-war sales trip to Saudi Arabia and struck a bonanza within weeks. Bechtel contracted to build a major portion of the 1,068-mile Trans-Arabian Pipeline linking the oil fields of the Arabian Gulf to the Mediterranean. Starting in 1944, Bechtel designed and built a modern refinery at Ras Tanure, creating the foundation of a partnership with Saudi Arabia that would last for decades. Steve forged a solid working relationship with King Saud, his son Prince Faisal and their advisers.

Another key development was Steve's – and thereafter Steve Bechtel, Jnr's – commitment to nuclear power. Steve Senior was convinced nuclear power would revolutionize electric power generation and he wanted a lion's share of it. Bechtel joined with several utilities to form the Nuclear Power Group which, in 1955, approached the US Atomic Energy Commission to construct the groundbreaking Dresden nuclear plant in Illinois. Construction began in early 1957 and was completed in 1959. It was generally accepted that Dresden did more to establish commercial nuclear power in the USA than any other project. Bechtel went on to be the leading builder of nuclear plants in the USA and many other countries. Much later, in 1979, they were asked to take on the daunting task of cleaning up the damaged Unit 2 at the Three Mile Island plant, which had been designed and built by other companies. A partial reactor meltdown had been caused by a valve failure and an operator error. Although the damage and radioactivity beyond the periphery of the plant was minimal, the impact of the accident on public opinion was devastating and proved a serious setback to the nuclear industry.

It would take a volume of this book to cover the development of Bechtel during Steve Bechtel Jnr's reign. Suffice to say there was rapid global exposure in the now familiar fields – nuclear energy, pipelines, oil production and refining, mining and metals, rapid-transit systems, hotels and liquefied natural gas. It is recognized that in less than two decades he had doubled the size and profitability of the organization that his forebears had taken sixty years to build.

Another commendable aspect of Bechtel's activities was the influential relationship they had with various US governments. A striking example was when Ronald Reagan became President. He invited two members of the Bechtel executive team, George Shulz and Casper Weinberger, to join his government, not as junior ministers, but in two key roles with Cabinet status. George Shulz, after a distinguished role in government, returned to Bechtel as an advisory director. He made regular visits to the UK and I accompanied him on discussions with clients and politicians, who were most anxious to hear his views. One discussion which stands out in my memory was on a Saturday morning with Ken Clarke, then our Chancellor of the Exchequer. They philosophized together for over an hour and when we left the Treasury, George Shulz volunteered the view: 'That is prime minister material if I ever saw it!'

Turning specifically to the UK, in 1979 Bechtel Ltd, under the leadership of John Neerhout, set about winning major contracts for oil and gas in the UK and Europe. When the price of crude oil rose to $40 a barrel, finding new sources of oil and gas became an attractive economic prospect and there were even fears that the price was headed for $100. With Europe desperately seeking indigenous energy sources, the North Sea, with its known but untapped deposits of oil and gas, became the world's most promising area for new exploration. Signing a contract to develop the Argyll Field in 1972, Bechtel entered North Sea history and confirmed its role as a leader in petroleum-production technology. Three years later Bechtel was at work on three large North Sea platforms for projects in the Argyll, Piper and Claymore fields, and also became involved in the Norwegian section of the North Sea with the Guillfaks A platform.

I joined Bechtel Ltd In January 1991, much in awe of the group's distinguished history. I soon visited the group's headquarters in San Francisco to meet Steve Bechtel, Jnr, his son, Riley, and other members of the senior team. I was talking to Steve when his secretary entered and announced that the Governor of the Bank of England was on the phone. I was then on the Court of the Bank and assumed that

Robin Leigh-Pemberton was chasing me, but the secretary said, 'No, he wishes to speak to Mr Bechtel.' Steve switched on the phone so that I could hear the conversation, and the gist of Robin's message was that the banks which were financing the Channel Tunnel were not willing to invest any more money in the project unless Bechtel took over the management role. Steve looked at me and I nodded, and he gave Robin a qualified 'yes'. He then said to me: 'There is only one man who can do the job and that is John Neerhout.' By then John had returned from London to San Francisco as Executive Vice-President of Bechtel Group. John did not hesitate a minute when he was asked to delegate his corporate responsibilities and become Chief Executive of Eurotunnel, the owner-developer of the Channel Tunnel. I was amazed at the speed with which this most important opportunity was resolved – in stark contrast with what would have happened in most major companies.

The Channel Tunnel project embraced a consortium of five British and five French companies and John Neerhout, with a small team of Bechtel veterans, was faced with the task of turning round the enterprise's failing engineering and construction effort. It was an enormously intricate project, involving two languages, two governments, three national railways, numerous subcontractors and a syndicate of 220 banks. There is no doubt that Neerhout will always be a revered name in the London office.

When I took over as Chairman, Ken Turnbull was the Managing Director – a highly experienced and competent operator who had been schooled in a wide range of activities on both sides of the Atlantic and in the People's Republic of China where he had been Bechtel's senior executive in the mid-1980s. He was supported by an excellent group of managers who covered the whole range of Bechtel's skills.

In the Bechtel office we continued to manage UK projects and also contributed to group activities. In the UK, in addition to the Channel Tunnel, we were later responsible for providing construction management help to London's Docklands in transforming a decrepit waterfront area on the Thames into a third city centre. We also managed the Limehouse Link project and John Major performed the opening ceremony in May 1993. Later we took over the construction management of the faltering Jubilee Line, which was completed well on time.

Elsewhere we made a major contribution to building a 140-mile section of Turkey's transnational highway system linking Europe and Asia. Being involved in building the new underground system in Athens caused me an embarrassing moment. Waiting to join a cruise, Joyce and I were staying one night in the Hotel Grande Bretagne and in the square below our bedroom one of the underground shafts was being sunk. It was very noisy and difficult to sleep. Joyce said I should ring the hotel manager and get it stopped, but I finally persuaded her of my conflict of interest.

In June 1990 Riley Bechtel took over the leadership from his father and another distinguished era for Bechtel followed. In August 1990 Saddam Hussein invaded neighbouring Kuwait and within days of the attack, Iraq took 109 Bechtel employees and their dependants hostage. In September ten Bechtel employees – three Americans and seven British nationals, who had taken refuge in their embassies along with their colleagues still trapped in Iraq – were snared by Iraqi immigration authorities, who lured them out by insisting that they appear person-ally to secure exit visas for their wives. When they left their embassy compounds, they were immediately swept up, taken to a facility on the outskirts of Baghdad and held there. Thanks to Riley Bechtel and the London office's efforts, every Bechtel person was eventually got safely out of Iraq before the Allies launched their assault to liberate Kuwait.

In 1991, in the aftermath of the Gulf War, Bechtel, under the over-all leadership of Riley, led the efforts to put out 650 oil well fires and rebuild Kuwait's oil industry. An estimated 70 million barrels of thick crude had spewed on to the desert floor, forming lethal lakes hiding unexploded ordnance. To borrow a phrase, Kuwait had become 'hell with the lid off'. This was probably the most daunting task Bechtel had ever faced and the London office played an important role in the group effort. Bechtel's assignment was to recruit, sustain and manage the workforce of 10,000 needed to extinguish the fires and restore petro-leum production. One immediate problem was how to house this army of workers and two old cruise liners were hired from Greece to accom-modate 2,000 of them.

Some experts estimated that it would take as long as five years simply to control the fires, but under Bechtel's guidance this was achieved in eight months. Controlling the wells so quickly saved the Kuwait Oil Co. billions of dollars in irreplaceable resources that otherwise would have gone up in smoke. Also the people of Kuwait and neighbouring countries were spared months, perhaps years, of severe air pollution and disruption. It had been anticipated that the costs of the operation could be as high as $100 billion but the final figure of reconstruction was less than £5 billion, which owed much to the skill, ingenuity, dedication and courage of Bechtel's people.

One aspect of the Bechtel operation which never ceased to amaze me was the way managers and their families were willing, at the drop of a hat, to move halfway across the world if the business required it. Kuwait was no exception and there was a management team of 1,500 quickly in place. I could not help comparing this with my experience of asking people to move in UK industrial companies. Even moving from Harrogate to London might lead to protracted negotiations.

From mid-1993, Joyce suffered from ovarian cancer, and it became increasingly difficult for me to fulfil my obligations with two part-time roles. With the greatest reluctance I therefore had to retire from Bechtel Limited.

Wasserstein Perella: 1991–9

It was a pleasure to be involved with Bruce Wasserstein and Jeffrey Rosen again after our fruitful relationship during my ICI days in New York. I became the non-executive Chairman in April 1991. Peter Levene joined later in the summer as Deputy Chairman and Jim Downing was Managing Director. We were essentially a merger and acquisition boutique, charged not only with doing deals in the UK but also focusing on cross-border acquisitions in Europe. Peter Levene and I had complementary business experience, and he was particularly strong in the defence industry, having been the Government's defence procurement chief, so much so that he had a secondary role in the USA as a managing director with responsibility there, too, for defence affairs. Jeffrey Rosen was our colleague in New York to whom we reported and from my point of view, recognizing our earlier relationship in my ICI days, this was a very beneficial and welcome arrangement.

In the high-stakes world of mergers and acquisitions, Bruce Wasserstein had become a living legend. He became known as 'Bid 'em up' Bruce because of his ability to get the best price for the firms he was selling. By 1998 he had over a thousand deals under his belt, including many of the largest – for example, the Time/Warner deal in 1989 and the KKR acquisition of RJR Nabasco in 1988, which was then the largest deal of all time and was subsequently translated into the film *Barbarians at the Gate*. Bruce wrote a book in 1998, *The Big Deal*, which covers the battle for the control of leading American corporations during this hectic period.

Bruce was in the news again recently, when he sold Wasserstein Perella to Dresdner Kleinwort Benson, from which he personally banked $600 million. Within a year he again profited hugely from Allianz's takeover of Dresdner. The German insurer, however, went back on a promise to establish an independent investment bank, which Bruce was to lead. David Weill of Lazards, knowing Bruce was understandably unhappy with the situation, approached him to become their leader. He has already surrounded himself with many 'old hands' from Wasserstein and I believe that this stage of Bruce's career will add even more lustre to his name.

Bruce is a fascinating character. I have never met anyone with a sharper analytical mind. He also has an encyclopaedic knowledge of the widest range of businesses and could converse in depth with our varied clients at any level with total authority. There were some critics who claimed he was not quite so strong as a people manager, but in his original highly successful venture with Joe Perella, he had a partner who was very complementary and provided all the charm that was needed.

When we were visiting a client together, in the car *en route* he would ask me questions about the people we were to meet and the current state of their businesses, but sometimes he would fail to inform me of any of his earlier involvements. A classic example was breakfast with Rick Greenbury, the Chairman of Marks & Spencer. The discussion was developing well when the subject of Brooks Bros, which M &

S had bought to develop their business in the US, came up. Much to my surprise Bruce suddenly said: 'I was on the sell-side of that deal, and you could have bought it for less than half the $750 million you paid.' I fully expected Rick to explode, but he said it was not his fault, blaming Derek Raynor, Marcus Sieff and Michael Sieff.

Bruce has always supported the Democratic Party and before the last US election Bill Clinton asked him to run a fund-raising dinner at his lovely home at East Hampton on Long Island. Attendees were asked to pay $25,000 a plate for the privilege. Jeffrey Rosen attended and gave me a run down on what happened. Understandably, security was extremely tight: gunmen were sited all round the perimeter of the estate and frogmen swam in Long Island Sound to protect the approach from the beach. Bruce's neighbour was Billy Joel, the pop-star, and if they were both in residence on Sundays he regularly came through their communal hedge to have a drink with Bruce who, on this occasion, rang him to say it would not be appropriate today, as he would probably be shot! Billy Joel decided to hire a bicycle and rode down his drive, along the main road and up Bruce's drive, where he queued in the line of stretch limousines which were bringing the well-heeled investment bankers to the party.

Wasserstein Perella was very different from my previous roles and it took a little time before I felt I could make a contribution. We had established our London office in Park Place and our immediate task was to build an effective team. I was pleasantly surprised with the ease with which we could recruit high-quality graduates. We had already taken on a capable group of experienced performers headed by Jim Downing in the key role of managing director.

The prime role of Peter Levene and myself was to expand our ever-increasing number of clients in the UK and Europe and in the process, where appropriate, to bring Bruce Wasserstein, Jeffrey Rosen and other New York colleagues into the discussions to emphasize what the group had to offer. There is no doubt that most new potential clients, despite having long-standing commitments to other investment banks, welcomed these approaches and gave us a good hearing.

Under the dynamic leadership of Jim Downing we were quickly involved in merger activity, in 1991 being involved in defending

Ultramar against a hostile bid from LASMO. In 1992 Wassall made a hostile bid for Evode and Jim Downing and Robert Easton were the main team leaders on the successful defence. In 1994 we advised SmithKline Beecham on acquiring Sterling Winthrop, a subsidiary of Eastman Kodak. Also in 1994, we sold SmithKline Beecham's North America consumer health business of Sterling Winthrop to Bayer AG. All these transactions were in the region of $3 billion.

We were also active in Italy. IRI, the state-owned holding company, invited us to help sell SME (GS Group's supermarkets and the motor-way Autogrill's restaurant chain), which went to a consortium of the Benetton family, Movenpick and others. In 1995 we were involved in our first Japanese deal with Richoh's acquisition of Gestetner.

Another interesting development in 1992 extended our activities into Russia and Eastern Europe. Michael Alexander, who joined as Deputy Chairman to spearhead this new initiative, had the ideal credentials of a distinguished Foreign Office and ambassadorial career. Among his posts were Private Secretary (Overseas Affairs) to Margaret Thatcher, our Ambassador in Vienna and ultimately Ambassador to NATO. This development proved more difficult and demanding than we had anticipated, but before Michael retired in 1997, he had estab-lished our presence in Kiev in 1992 as Kinto Securities, of which he became Chairman, and in 1995 became co-founder and Deputy Chairman of Capital SA Bucharest, and also co-founder of Sector Capital, Moscow.

In 1994 Peter Levene decided to move on and became Chairman of Canary Wharf and in 1998/9 he was the renowned Lord Mayor of London. His exit was followed some months later by Jim Downing who moved to Lehman Bros, and this caused a temporary slow-down in our progress. But this was reversed immediately in early 1996 when Howard Covington joined us from Warburgs. His arrival gave the company a real shot in the arm. We had already overgrown our office in Park Place and moved to more spacious surroundings in No. 3, Burlington Gardens.

Among many other innovations, Howard introduced a novel recruitment technique. When visiting, say, Oxford or Cambridge University, he would allow potential recruits to meet and discuss with some of our recent entrants their early experience of working in Wasserstein Perella. There is no doubt this proved beneficial.

Our analysts were an extremely good team, who did not have to share the problems of their opposite numbers in the all-embracing investment banks, where there is an inbuilt conflict between supporting their company clients and their role as investment advisers.

There is no doubt that the tempo of the business improved sharply from Howard's arrival. Among the many deals we did, the following are worthy of special mention:

- There had been a rush of US utilities into the UK market and in 1996 we represented Virginia-based Dominion Resources in a $2.5 billion acquisition of the UK's East Midlands Electricity.
- In 1997 Wasserstein Perella, at group level, participated in a groundbreaking deal – the merger of Swiss Bank and the Union of Switzerland to form the United Bank of Switzerland (UBS), which would become the world's second largest bank. The size of the transaction was $25 billion.
- Also in 1997, we advised British Aerospace, who bought Marconi Electronics System, a division of GEC, for £12.8 billion.
- In 1999 we advised NTL Inc, who bought Cablecom Holding AG (Switzerland), which was owned by Swisscom, Siemens AG and VEBA, for $3.7 billion.

My impression of investment bankers is that most of them are brilliant individualists, but as their achievements are highly focused over a short time-scale they rarely develop any significant management skills and would certainly have difficulty in moving into an equivalent job in any major industrial management structure. Moreover, I believe that if there were a celestial job assessor looking down on the global scene, the rewards pattern of industrial jobs and those in investment banking would be sharply inverted on any well-based criteria. I much enjoyed this late exposure in rounding off my career, but I was equally clear that I could never have made investment banking my life career.

151

My final involvement in Wasserstein Perella was my most exciting. We were asked by Wal-Mart in 1999 to approach Asda to see if they would welcome a bid for their company, even though they were well advanced with their announced plans to merge with Kingfisher. I rang Archie Norman, then Chairman of Asda, and asked if we might have a discussion with him. He was very reluctant and explained that he was being bombarded with similar requests. How did he know our approach was genuine and not an exploratory one? I replied that what we wished to discuss would almost certainly excite him and he would regret not meeting us. So a date was arranged. The *Sunday Telegraph* reported as follows: 'Early last month a pair of well-heeled business-men, Lord Haslam and Howard Covington of Wasserstein Perella, visited Archie Norman and their short meeting would change British retailing forever.'

This was an over-dramatic statement but Howard and I quickly real-ized, once Archie was sure our approach was for real, that we did not have a selling job to do, as he so obviously preferred the Wal-Mart option to merging with Kingfisher. We happily reported back to our US clients and as I was due to retire a few days later, it was good to depart on this high note. Howard Covington, working with his New York colleagues along with top executives of Wal-Mart, consummated the deal in about six weeks at a price of nearly $12 billion.

My retirement party from Wasserstein Perella at Spencer House was my best ever. Bruce and Jeffrey indicated that I should not confine my invitations to our clients, but should focus on my closest friends. Scanning the room as I was making my brief farewell speech, I could see friends from virtually every stage of my varied career and I found it all quite moving.

British Occupational Health Research Foundation: 1994–2000

My other rewarding involvement during this 'semi-retirement' period was my chairmanship of the newly formed British Occupational Health Research Foundation (BOHRF). It was the brainchild of Christopher Lawrence-Jones, who was the Chief Medical Officer of ICI, and David McWilliam, who became the Director-General. Their philosophy was that the Medical Research Council dealt very effectively with the range of domestic diseases but there was no equivalent body covering industrial diseases.

When they asked me to become BOHRF Chairman in 1994 I readily accepted because during my period at British Coal we had lived through a period of massive claims for compensation for noise-induced hearing loss from miners. A surprising feature was that solicitors in many areas were openly advertising in the local press, virtually saying that they could get their clients compensation. I quickly became aware that there was little or no shared research on this topic and although other industries were receiving similar claims from their employees, there was no co-ordination on how to respond. Obviously some of these claims were valid, but others were not, and there was not enough scientific evidence to differentiate, hence there was little or no option but to pay out on every claim.

To finance the activities of BOHRF we had to raise funds through a patrons' programme. Among the range of patrons were BP, the Colt Foundation, Glaxo Wellcome, ICI, Marks & Spencer, Scottish & Newcastle, Shell UK, Unilever and Whitbread. We also enjoyed active support from the TUC and the Health and Safety Executive.

Our projects were carried out by universities and other appropriate research organizations and covered a wide range of problems, including a study of vibration white finger syndrome, mental ill health in the UK workforce and osteoarthritis of the knee caused by heavy lifting. We also engaged in project financing, jointly with a single company, to sponsor a particular project – a classic example being a study which Blue Circle undertook on back pain guidelines.

Michael Ladenburg took over as Director from David McWilliam in 1998, about the time when it was becoming clear that we could not meet all the increasing demands on our funds. In 2000 he recommended that we should merge with the Faculty of Occupational Medicine and this happened in December, in line with my intention to retire from BOHRF.

11
Educational Involvements

My prime involvements in the educational world were as Chairman of the Governors of Bolton School from 1990 to 1997 and as Chairman of the Council of Manchester Business School from 1985 to 1990.

Bolton School
Bolton School gave a marvellous start to my life and career and, having benefited from its commendable foundation policy of wide accessibility, I was delighted to have an opportunity to repay that debt.

The Leverhulme family were its greatest benefactors and a major objective of the first Lord Leverhulme, when he re-endowed the school, was that no Bolton child of academic potential should be excluded owing to family financial circumstances. About one-third of all pupils received support with their fees. He began the construction of the present splendid school buildings in 1924 and continued throughout the 1930s and after the war, when the main wings were completed. The Tillitson and Leigh-Bramwell families are among others who also made valuable contributions to the school's development and well-being.

In 1985, as President of the Old Boltonians' Association, I was asked to lay the foundation stone for a new sports hall and swimming pool. The building was opened next year by Philip Leverhulme who, following the family tradition, was Chairman of the Governors. When he decided to retire in 1990, Philip asked me to succeed him as

Chairman and I was delighted to accept.

In 1990 we launched the 'Funding the Future' programme, enabling the original swimming baths to be converted into a splendid new arts centre. A real highlight was when Princess Diana opened it in 1993. I was pleasantly surprised when she accepted the invitation, having only recently been in Bolton to open the new hospice, of which I am a patron, and making an early return visit was unlikely. She certainly had a marvellous touch in talking to the pupils and putting them at ease, making the day a great success for everyone. As we said farewell to her, two sixth-formers abseiled down the central tower and, much to her surprise and mine, rushed across and presented her with a box of Cadbury's Milk Tray!

In 1995 we acquired a 300-acre estate, Patterdale Hall, at the southern end of Ullswater, to provide spacious facilities for groups of pupils in all kinds of country pursuits. In 1997 we started to build on the campus a high-class nursery for the town and the first children arrived in mid-1998. It was also designed to generate a considerable profit to fund extra scholarships.

As I explained in Chapter 1, when I was a pupil at the school there was a Berlin Wall attitude of keep the boys' and girls' divisions totally separate, and elements of this still persisted with the governing body having separate committees for each. These were quickly abandoned and we began integrating the two divisions, focusing initially on sixth-form activities because it was regarded as essential to create the right environment for pupils' maturing needs. We also had to keep abreast of all aspects of information technology and provided up-to-date computer systems, so vital for every pupil's education.

The school's performance was outstanding during this period, both on the sporting field and in examination results. In the annual summary of A Level results in the *Daily Telegraph*, the two divisions were quoted separately, but it was not unusual for one of them to be in the top ten of all UK schools. In 1997 the boys' division was commendably ranked sixth, higher than any other North-west school.

These results were a reflection of the outstanding performance of the Headmaster, Alan Wright, and of the two headmistresses of my period, Margaret Spurr and Jane Panton. Alan, who will have retired when this book is published, was Headmaster of the boys' division for sixteen years, leading and motivating a talented team of teaching staff. Margaret Spurr was Headmistress for fifteen years – a brilliant leader who became a prominent figure on the wider educational scene. On retirement in 1994 she was in great demand and among other activities became a BBC governor. I was apprehensive about her departure because finding a successor would be a formidable task. We appointed Jane Panton, who quickly made her mark and, with the support of a dedicated teaching staff, has led the division to even greater heights. The school's performance was also enhanced by the excellent team of ancillary staff, ably led by Robin Senior, the Bursar and Treasurer.

The governors were an outstanding group of dedicated colleagues who served the school extremely well by pursuing progressive policies, making my role as Chairman both enjoyable and satisfying. During these years, however, a dark cloud emerged, with the Labour Party adopting a policy that if they came to power they would abandon the Assisted Places Scheme. Between the two divisions we had 2,000 pupils, of whom some 600 depended on the scheme, which enabled us to fulfil our mission of providing education for any Bolton child of academic potential from poorer families.

When the Labour Party came to power in 1997 the announcement we were dreading was made, but it was still a surprise to me, as it did not seem to fit the concepts of New Labour. Bolton had a population of about 200,000 people, equivalent to 50,000 families, many of them Labour supporters with high hopes of their children becoming beneficiaries of our 600 assisted places. I spoke on this topic in the House of Lords, explaining that we would have no difficulty at all in filling the school with fee-paying pupils. If we did so, however, where would those talented 600 pupils whose parents could not afford our fees be educated in Bolton?

We decided not to follow the easy option but to continue to observe the Leverhulme concept of maintaining our intake of pupils from poorer families. This involved stepping up our fundraising activities to support scholarships and bursaries. We also increased our commercial activities by, for example, leasing out the Arts Centre at weekends for weddings and other events. The new nursery, too, soon became a useful contributor. The response from all our funds and resources, including the old boys' and girls' associations, was commendable.

Looking back, I am sure the Labour Party realized that they had made a mistake by abolishing rather than modifying the Assisted Places Scheme. Commendably, my close friend, Robert Ogden, has been showing them the effective way forward for the past four years. I first met Robert when I was Chairman of British Coal. My predecessors and their technical advisers had decided that all the coal to be extracted from the new Selby mining complex would be so clean no washery plant was needed. However, at the end of the first month of supplying the mighty Drax Power Station Walter Marshall, the CEGB Chairman, rang to say they could not use the Selby coal unless it was washed! This seemed like an immediate catastrophe as it would take at least a year to build a conventional washery at the complex. We were aware that Robert and one of his cohorts, Jack Hanson, were reclaiming old coal tips using mobile washery plants, so washing Selby coal would be relatively easy. We invited them to help with our immediate problem, which they did with flying colours!

I am a great admirer of Robert, who is the most modest entrepreneur and benefactor I have ever met. In 1999 he established a scholarship scheme for pupils in the forty-seven schools in the Barnsley, Doncaster and Rotherham areas to continue their education through the sixth form and at the University of Leeds. The pupils chosen were those who might not, for social or financial reasons, otherwise continue education beyond GCSE. A full-time administrator had to be established at the University of Leeds, not only to administer the scheme but to help select the entrants in consultation with the local education authorities, the vice chancellors and Robert himself. While David Blunkett was Secretary of State for Education he had many discussions with Robert and was a keen supporter of this experiment.

Each year forty scholars are chosen and now about 160 benefit from his scheme, which provides £500 in the first sixth-form year, £1,000 in the second and £2,000 a year at university. Robert's annual commitment is in excess of £300,000, with firm plans to expand. Other benefactors have begun to follow his example and, most importantly, the Government is beginning to take faltering steps in this direction.

Robert has also been a generous and enthusiastic supporter of a wide range of charities, including the Macmillan Cancer Relief Fund, the Home Farm Trust, the National Autistic Society, the Prince of Wales Hospice at Pontefract and the Northern Racing College. He is equally generous in his hospitality at his homes at Sickling Hall in Yorkshire and at Cap Ferrat in the south of France. With a deep interest in horse racing he has regularly been the leading owner during the National Hunt season, providing other delightful venues for entertaining friends.

Robert asked me to say a few words at the luncheon following his knighthood investiture by the Queen, and I made the point that his friends found it impossible to reciprocate his gracious hospitality. My wife Elizabeth thought otherwise and made the special effort of inviting Robert and his partner Jennifer to attend one of her conferences at Pentonville Prison. Robert arrived in his Rolls-Royce and caused some consternation in the prison as I believe he was assumed to be the Mafia boss from the East End visiting his flock!

Throughout a business career which embraced not only the exploitation of coal tips and land reclamation, estate development and property investment, he also embraced substantial interests in transport, heavy construction equipment, civil engineering and quarrying. It was this eye for an opportunity, allied to an overriding determination to succeed, which led to his becoming one of the most successful businessmen of his generation. Not bad for a boy who left school at fourteen and worked as a farm labourer until he was called up for National Service! A truly remarkable man.

Manchester Business School

In 1985 a former ICI colleague, Rab Telfer, who was Director of the Manchester Business School, invited me to become Chairman of their council and I readily accepted. The Council had some outstanding people, including Peter Middleton, who became Chairman of Barclays Bank, Don Cruickshank, now Chairman of the London Stock Exchange, and Anne Muller, then the most senior female civil servant, along with talented professors from the business school and the university.

We were quite pleased with the progress we were making, but I quickly realized that we were not keeping pace with the development and quality of the London Business School, established by government at the same time. One of the reasons was that we were accountable through Manchester University, which led to unhelpful conflicts and wrangling, whereas London was self-contained and answerable directly to the Government.

In 1989 Tom Cannon took over from Rab as Director and the following year our twenty-fifth anniversary celebrations were led by the Duke of Kent, with John King, British Airways Chairman, and John Harvey-Jones, by then a TV personality with his *Troubleshooter* programmes, as the two main speakers.

I was to retire in 1990 and be succeeded by Dennis Landau. I was pleased that our efforts over the years to establish a free-standing and self-contained Manchester Business School seemed to be bearing fruit. The announcement came in 1993 when the Vice-Chancellor of the university, Martin Harris, and the Principal of UMIST, Harold Hankins, made a joint statement that new arrangements would bring together the Manchester Business School, the Management School at UMIST and the university's Department of Accounting and Finance, creating a very strong organization which could compete internationally for management and business education. Sadly this pronouncement led to a federal structure of the three separate elements. John Arnold, the present Dean of the business school, assures me that it is a very beneficial step forward, but I still believe the business school will never fulfil its objective of competing with the leaders like London, INSEAD, and others in Europe and the USA unless it is truly independent and self-contained. For example, within the federal organization I assume the salary structure will be the same as the university and UMIST, but to put the business school in the top league they need international staff of the highest calibre and will have to pay them accordingly.

12
Wives and Family

I would like to mention two exceptional wives, as they reflect the differing roles which have evolved over the past fifty years.

Joyce and I married in 1947 and decided not to have children for five years so that we could get on our feet – but Roger, our eldest son, entered the world some eleven months later! Joyce became a classic 'company' wife, as my ICI career involved us in many moves with ten homes in thirty-six years. Perhaps her most stressful time was when I was travelling the world as a technical service engineer for Nobel Division, often being away for a few weeks at a time. The worst experience was when I was in South America for three months and my mother had a thrombosis. Joyce temporarily returned from Scotland with Roger to our Bolton family home to look after both my parents. She accepted all these trials and tribulations with equanimity and never complained.

Conversely, in my more senior ICI posts, she greatly enjoyed travelling with me on my many visits in the UK and overseas. She readily reciprocated by entertaining wives and families of directors and managers of our overseas companies when they came to the UK. I believe that this 'ambassadorial' role, which was performed by Lorna Pennock, Chris Duncan and many other ICI wives, went a long way to developing a family spirit in the company's top echelons. It is difficult to put a value on this, but I am sure it was a positive feature in the strength and well-being of the company.

Our two sons, Roger and Nigel, got a good start educationally as they both attended Glasgow Academy, but in 1961 it became clear that we would not be returning to Scotland and we decided to move them to London. I had great difficulty in relocating them, but this changed suddenly when I applied for a place for Nigel at Westminster Under School. When I arrived at the school the Headmaster, Mr Campbell, was waiting at the door; we went to his study and, much to my amazement, he said, 'When would you wish your son to join us?' I replied, 'Don't you want to see him?' And he said: 'No, you did my son a good turn and I would like to reciprocate.' I tried hard to remember ever having helped a young Campbell, and eventually it came back to me that I had met him at a party at our Glasgow sales office. He had behaved rather badly that night, but I was otherwise impressed with him and invited him to lunch soon after to give him some fatherly advice. I had apparently applied to the school on ICI notepaper and the Headmaster presumably mentioned my name to his son, who must have given me a special chit! Nigel was very happy at Westminster Under School and eventually became Head Boy.

Roger was to take an examination for entrance to Westminster School. His mother took him to Glasgow Airport for an early-morning flight. She had arranged for him to be met at Heathrow, but that was unfortunately fogbound and the plane landed at Gatwick. Nevertheless, he managed to find his way to the school, but arrived just as the examination was finishing. There was a school concert that evening and parents were already ringing in to say that because of the fog they would not be able to make it. The school was therefore surprised that Roger had arrived unaided from Glasgow and after a brief interview they decided he should have a place. Both he and eventually Nigel became weekly boarders at Westminster, coming home after games on Saturday evening and returning on Monday morning. Roger rowed for the school at Henley and Nigel played football for the school XI.

On returning from the USA in 1981, which incidentally Joyce regarded as one of the happiest two years of her life, we bought a house at Wentworth, Surrey. I had known Michael Sieff very well during my ICI Fibres days, but had no idea I was about to be his immediate neighbour. From the outset he and his wife, Elizabeth, were extremely generous neighbours and through them we quickly made many local friends.

In 1984 Michael became ill and his health gradually deteriorated, but Elizabeth, with her background in nursing, could not have done more to help and support him. She took him from specialist to specialist, from hospital to hospital, in the hope that he could be cured. Michael also liked her to stay with him overnight. This was not difficult to arrange in hospitals like the Wellington, but even in NHS hospitals she would sleep on a camp bed next to him, coming home during the day to look after her two young children, Daniel and Elizabeth Anne, who had a nanny but obviously still needed their mother's care and attention. We observed all this happening.

Sadly Michael died in 1987. Elizabeth found it extremely difficult to continue to live in their home and eventually moved to a new house, but to our delight still at Wentworth, so we continued to see her and the children regularly.

In mid-1993 Joyce was diagnosed with ovarian cancer. She had an exploratory operation in the autumn and it was decided that chemotherapy was the preferred treatment, with a protracted series on a monthly basis. After each treatment she was off colour for three days or so, but she was soon able to behave normally and each month we headed for Cannes for a long weekend. We were very encouraged that our medical team believed there was optimism the outcome would be positive. But it was not to be; in mid-November 1994 she had a consultation at the Royal Marsden Hospital and it was found that the cancer had spread to her bowel.

She was operated on in early December, but despite the hospital's well-deserved reputation, I believe she was an exception because I felt the operation was botched. While she was in the recovery room it was suggested, to my amazement, that I should ask my immediate family to join me and stay overnight. Joyce survived the night, and I was so unhappy at the way she had been treated that I was determined, as soon as she was fit enough to travel by ambulance, to transfer her to Runnymede Hospital, where she earlier had treatment, and in whose medical staff we had great confidence. Moving on 4 January she was welcomed and immediately responded to the congenial ambience.

The medical team confirmed that her condition was probably terminal but they were determined to make it possible for her to come home. Much to her delight she did so in early February. She passed away on 29 March, after eight weeks at our Surrey home, where she was able to walk about in her beloved garden and see her spring flowers bloom. She had been a wonderful wife and so ended nearly forty-eight years of a perfect marriage.

After a distressing period of mourning, I realized that a bachelor's life was not for me and I began to welcome invitations from lady friends. It amazed me that Elizabeth Sieff had not remarried, and it seemed almost preordained that we would come together. I was highly delighted when she accepted my marriage proposal. It is difficult to conceive how anyone can have had two more perfect wives than me.

Joyce and Elizabeth had many similar characteristics and in earlier days Elizabeth, too, could have been a fine 'company wife'. She soon decided to develop the niche she had carved out for herself prior to Michael's death. In 1985 Jasmine Beckford, a black three-year-old child, was murdered by her stepfather, Maurice Beckford – who had also been a victim of physical abuse as a child – after he had tortured her for many months. This happened despite the child being on the at risk register with the local authority, and the nursery she attended being under the care of the local council. It seemed, possibly because of poor management and inappropriate concern over confidentiality, that this little girl died an appalling death. Out of this avoidable tragedy the Michael Sieff Foundation was born. Elizabeth was so moved by this tragic story that she decided to take action. Encouraged by her husband, she organized a three-day residential conference of practitioners and policymakers with the objective of improving communications and practices so that such tragic incidents would be minimized. The eminent QC Louis Blom-Cooper, who had scrutinized the case, and Norman Fowler, then the Secretary of State for Health, were present.

After Michael died, Elizabeth formed the charity in his name and asked me to become a trustee and later, the Chairman. The aim then and now is to help the professionals to support children in need. The foundation holds one-day conferences and an annual three-day meeting addressing all these related issues. We believe we were the first organization to hold multi-disciplinary conferences attracting civil servants from all the different departments concerned and also children's charities and many others whose concerns focus on child care and young people. This was an early example of 'joined-up government'.

I believe that over the last sixteen years the foundation has made many notable contributions to the well-being of a host of children and young people. The following are some examples:

- We have lobbied for young people with criminal records to be able to join the Army and some forty have now become soldiers. We have made a landmark video informing young people in prison about industries, companies and other organizations who are willing to give them a second chance by way of training and jobs on release. There has been a positive response from forty companies and the number is rising.

- The 1989 Children's Act's accompanying document was finalized at our annual conference.

- The training of social and psychiatric workers has been addressed and improved.

- There are continuing improvements for children in care as a result of delegates urging accredited professionalism for the residential care service.

- Most of all we have helped organizations to look at their own practices and procedures to improve the care of children in the UK and overseas.

- Following the Belgian paedophile scandal we ran an international conference – partly funded by the King Baudouin Foundation – which had far-reaching ramifications on this infamous subject.

- Our conference on sexual abuse, we were told, was pivotal in the outcome of the Stockholm Conference on the Rights of the Child. Our report was translated into the three working languages.

- The foundation's main achievement has been to act as a catalyst by bringing together people of different persuasions, who would not normally meet, to improve their practices by working more closely together.

Over the years my admiration of what Elizabeth and the foundation have achieved grows and grows and her enthusiasm and her energy know no bounds. Striking a humorous note when introducing her at a recent meeting, I explained that there are special administrative stresses when, as Chairman, you are also sleeping with your Chief Executive – and, looking back on dealing with Mr Scargill in the coal industry for five years, now seems relatively simple and straightforward!

Returning to the family, Roger graduated from Dundee University with a geology degree and Nigel followed my example with a degree at Birmingham University, but in his case in the law faculty.

Soon after Roger graduated he married Astrid, a Norwegian girl, at the renowned Maria Kirken in Bergen in January. Though we tried to persuade them to wait for a more congenial time of year, I will never forget the scene as we emerged from the church: snow all around, a clear black sky with the stars and the moon shining brilliantly – just like a film set. Roger had a string of jobs in the UK, including a period on a Ford management scheme. He decided to use his geological skills, however, and they moved to the Copper Belt in Zambia, making their home there in Luanshaya. They certainly enjoyed their lifestyle, though it created an unusual travel problem for me. Whether we were on a trip to the USA or India, Joyce thought a diversion via Zambia to see her first grandchild – Sara born in 1975 – was perfectly normal and acceptable. However, the family's lifestyle came to an abrupt end. The Copper Belt had been suffering for some time from bandits crossing the border from the Congo and causing mayhem. One night two of Roger's closest friends were shot dead when leaving a local cinema. He decided enough was enough and they took the reluctant decision to return to the UK.

They went to live near Cambridge and Roger took up a post with consultants advising on the use of computers in improving manufacturing processes – then in its relative infancy. Since then he has had a series of jobs in a variety of high-tech industries. Sadly, in 1992 he and his wife Astrid divorced, but she still resides in Cambridge so their daughters, Sara and Roberta, have ready access to both their mother and father. Sara took a degree at Bristol and managed the shop in the Fitzwilliam Museum, Cambridge. Roberta graduated from Sussex University.

After graduation, Nigel took up a job with one of the major London solicitors, Radcliffes. He seemed to be making reasonable progress, but it soon became obvious he wished to set up his own operation and in 1992 he and a colleague, Richard Payne, left Radcliffes and established the law firm Haslam and Payne. It was a courageous step to take as competing with the renowned and established companies in London was going to be a tough challenge by any standards, but they have been successful. Nigel had a string of girl friends but one was our outstanding favourite, Alison. We were delighted when they married in 1988 and went on to present Joyce and me with two delightful grandchildren, Sophie and James, who are both at school.

On marrying Elizabeth it was an added bonus to inherit a stepson, Daniel Sieff, who graduated in politics from Essex University, and a stepdaughter, Elizabeth Anne, who is finishing her education at the European Business School. Daniel worked in a laudable charity Training for Life, which provides training and job opportunities for the socially excluded, where he made a real impact. Daniel and Elizabeth Anne are nearly the same age as my eldest grandchildren and gratifyingly, although very different, they get on remarkably well together.

Overall my family life could hardly have been excelled.

13
Reflections

It is appropriate to round off the book by reflecting on my past involvements and by commenting on some current issues.

The Bank of England
I served on the Court of the Bank of England from 1985 to 1993 and it was a rewarding and illuminating experience. Robin Leigh-Pemberton was then Governor and Eddie George the Deputy Governor. The composition of the Court could not be faulted as the financial institutions, industry and the trade unions were all represented, along with the key bank officials. Even so, I felt that the balance of our discussions was too focused on financial aspects and potentially on the perils of inflation. We were usually considering circumstances which would arise two years hence but rarely was this matched with the actual outcome.

The threat of inflation, I believe, was consistently overstated then. Since the bank's Monetary Policy Committee (MPC) was launched, it has obviously done a commendable job in keeping inflation under control by meeting the 2.5 per cent target. The Chancellor of the Exchequer's remit refers to delivering price stability in this way and supporting the Government's economic policy, including objectives for growth and employment. But I feel the MPC should have been given more challenging terms of reference, because our currency has been consistently overvalued, leading to the contraction of our manufacturing industry and a deteriorating balance of payments. It seems untenable to put inflation on a unique pedestal. While it might remain the prime target, surely the MPC should have been given a broader remit embracing, for example, exchange rate management.

Moreover I cannot understand why the MPC does not have a press conference at the end of its monthly two-day meeting, rather than waiting for two weeks to publish the minutes and creating more speculation and uncertainty by announcing the members' voting performance. This confusion is compounded even more by the bank issuing its own inflation report every quarter.

The Euro

A lot of the problems encountered in the 1990s were blamed unfairly on our decision to join the Exchange Rate Mechanism (ERM) in 1991 and our humiliatingly ejection from it in 1992. As the other twelve nations demonstrated, there was nothing basically wrong with the ERM and the damage in the UK was essentially self-inflicted by entering at the ridiculously high rate of DM2.95 to the pound. This was to be expected because UK interest rates were then 5 per cent higher than in Germany and our inflation rate was running at nearly 10 per cent. Many industrialists were advocating figures of DM2.40 to DM2.50, but their views were ignored. Until mid-1996 the stability claimed by the Treasury and the Bank of England was being achieved, with the pound fluctuating between DM2.20 and DM2.60; but since mid-1996 the pound has taken off, reaching a peak of DM3.40 in 2001 and still hovering around DM3.15 just before the euro was introduced in January 2002.

We have voluntarily put ourselves back into a position even more dramatic than when we were relieved to be ejected. Can these wild gyrations in exchange rates be justified, having regard to the very adverse impact they continue to have on the UK's industrial strategies and exports?

Geoffrey Howe, in a recent article, highlighted that if we joined the euro at least 80 per cent of all trade by British businesses – in Britain as well as throughout the eurozone – would be carried out in one currency. Outside we might preserve our sovereignty but the real danger is that sterling will become the prime 'punchball currency' for speculators, bouncing as it is bound to do between the dollar and the Euro bloc. Geoffrey continued: 'As a former Chancellor I know how little control individual governments have over the value of their currencies. Margaret Thatcher spelt out the lesson we both learned, as together we watched the rate move within five years from $2.40 to the pound to near parity. "You can't buck the market" she once observed.' He added: 'I would shed few tears over the loss of this unmanageable aspect of sovereignty.'

In November 1997 Joel Barnett and I wrote a letter to the *Financial Times* headed 'Leisurely Steps towards EMU', urging that we should be courageous enough to join. I hope that soon after the five tests have been evaluated, the accelerator will be pressed and the date of the referendum announced. My perception is that most people who might vote 'no' still believe that we should remain members of the European Union (EU) and benefit from the single market. In my view this will not be the case. If we have a 'no' vote I am sure EU industrialists will pressure their governments into getting us rejoin the ERM. If we refuse, we could then be on the slippery slope leading to our with-drawal from the EU. Certainly any idea of renegotiating any EU constraints we did not like would still be so much hot air. Many eurosceptics would welcome this outcome. There is, however, a belief that this will not happen, because we buy as much from the other countries as we sell to them. This, too, is a false premiss. Those imports are spread over fourteen countries and on average represent 4 per cent of each one's exports, whereas our exports to the EU represent 55 per cent of our overseas trade. If tariffs were to be applied on our exports, then the other countries would have to make relatively small adjust-ments in their trading patterns to make up for any modest imports from the UK.

The eurosceptics also do not appear to recognize that the major global exporters in the UK are already increasingly asking their suppli-ers to quote them in euros; if the referendum led to a 'no' vote, then this trend would sharply accelerate. This approach would also ripple down through the business chains as each tier of suppliers would then call on their own suppliers to follow suit. Many small businesses could eventually face such demands, even though they are supplying only British manufacturers. It is understandable that passing exchange risk down the supply chain is a perfectly logical and legitimate thing to do.

Niall Fitzgerald, the Chairman of Unilever plc, is a strong supporter of the euro and their recent two annual reports gave performance in that currency. At the AGM some eurosceptic shareholders complained bitterly about this, but Niall responded by saying: 'We now do more business in euros than we do in dollars or pounds, and hence it is logical we should focus on the euro.'

Not many people realize that Denmark is still an ERM member and it is puzzling, with this tight constraint already existing, that people there have so far voted against adopting the euro. Clearly it was primarily the other aspects of being members of the EU the Danes were expressing concerns about and probably the question in their referendum should have been: 'Do you wish to remain in the EU or not?' For the same reason, the only honest referendum in the UK should be based on the same question, because withdrawal will be the most likely ultimate outcome of a 'no' vote on the euro.

There is no doubt, too, that inward investment in companies exporting to the EU would be even more at risk; our car industry is a classic example. Being already controlled by overseas companies, motor firms here are already phasing out their activities and this will surely escalate if we do not join the euro. Increasing amounts of recent inward investment have been in essentially domestic businesses – for example, our electricity and water industries and some of the prime hotel chains, including the Savoy. Does this mean they believe they can run these businesses better and more profitably than we can?

Our ability to run major global business is, I believe, still pre-eminent on the world scene. Shell, BP and Unilever are splendid examples, but during the last decade we have not built on this reputation. With the exception of the oil and pharmaceutical industries, we have not extended our global horizons in any substantial way. Nevertheless individual companies like Vodafone have also become significant global players. Conversely in retailing, with the exception of Tesco, we have tended to be in a withdrawing mode, with Marks & Spencer being a prime example.

The City is a further worry; none of the major investment banks is now British owned, having been taken over one by one by the Americans, the Swiss, the Germans or the Japanese. I have heard friends in these organizations say they believe this is fine because the City is well plugged into international developments. That may be so, but I wish at least some of the chairmen of these companies had the aspiration and determination to build their own European or global business. The commercial banks have shown little appetite for building global empires – with the exception of HSBC, for which we can hardly claim credit if we reflect on its history. I was based in New York when several British banks were having exploratory discussions with US units. Midland Bank made a bid for Crocker Bank, which turned out to be a disastrous US foray, and I believe this coloured the aspirations of other banks, who apparently decided not to pursue US targets.

Altogether the 1990s have not been a period to be very proud of either in the City or in industry, for expanding our businesses overseas at the rate we had previously established and sustained.

Unilever 1986-93

Soon after Mike Angus became Chairman of Unilever plc in 1986 he invited me to join as an advisory director, an invitation I was delighted to accept. Unilever was a complex company to manage because it also embraced Unilever N/V, whose Chairman was Floris Maljers. The board alternated meetings between London and Rotterdam, the only difference being that the resident chairman took the meeting. It was all impressively managed and seeing the executive directors responsible for their businesses only served to reinforce my view that the ICI approach to the role of their executive directors was much less effective. Another positive factor was the quality of the international advisory directors Unilever attracted, including the former Chairman of the Bundesbank, Otto Pohl, former President Francois Ortola of the European Commission, and former Ford Chairman Don Petersen.

In 1991 Unilever decided to establish a board audit committee and Mike Angus asked me to be the first Chairman. Among the members were two other international advisory directors, Romano

Prodi, now President of the European Commission, whose humour made even an audit committee enjoyable, and a recent Dutch finance minister, Otto Ruding. We were ably served by our auditors, Coopers & Lybrand. At that time the global scandal of bribery in business was at its height and we were charged with checking how our multitude of companies were behaving. This was not an easy assignment as some companies were operating in countries, including Latin America, where bribing suppliers was the norm. In fact, in some countries, companies formally indicated they would accept bribes and others declared they would not. Fortunately we found on the evidence available to us that all our companies were in the latter category.

Overall, Unilever was still building and extending its global business during this period at an impressive rate and at every board meeting the Chairman announced a string of proposed acquisitions and/or capital projects, which were rarely challenged by members. Altogether this spell on the Unilever board was one of the most educative periods of my life; my only regret is that it came so late in my career!

UK Energy Policy

Numerous policy reviews and statements have been made in recent months by the EU, the UK's Department of Trade and Industry (DTI) and, in February 2002, the all-embracing report *The Energy Review* from the Cabinet Office Performance and Innovation Unit (PIU), now called the Strategy Unit. These, along with occasional conflicting statements by ministers, mean that I am faced with commenting on a confused future picture.

The key factor is that, whichever report is followed, we shall be highly dependent on imported energy sources. You may remember my departing message to John Wakeham, referred to in Chapter 9, that we should preserve not less than forty low-cost pits which could give future access to all the vast resources of workable coal still existing in the country without the prohibitive costs of having to sink new shafts and build new surface plants. Sadly this level has long been breached and the number is now down to thirteen, with other closures being discussed.

The present pits, I believe, are capable of accessing about 150 million tonnes of coal resources. If the forty pits had been preserved, as we had recommended, more than a billion tonnes would be potentially available. In addition there are at least 300 million tonnes of opencast coal reserves in the UK. Germany and Spain decided that they would maintain substantial elements of their coal industries. Germany, for example, in the late 1980s was supporting its private coal industry by about £4 billion a year. These were direct cash payments to their electricity industry to compensate for the different cost of using German domestic coal, compared with the perceived price of delivered coal from international sources. In this period, every UK pit we closed had far better costs than the best pits in Germany. While German pits were virtually insulated from the impact of international imports, our coal industry suffered the full weight of imports coming into the country.

There is no doubt in my mind that we should plan for a resurgence of our coal industry and clearly this would have to be linked with investment in clean coal technology (CCT) at our elderly power stations. It is just fifteen years since I discussed the immediate need for this development with the Government and the European Commission. Brussels did support financially our experimental programme at Yorkshire's Grimethorpe Colliery, but we had to abandon it eventually for lack of future resources. Incidentally, producers have calculated that financial support for CCT plant would cost only 30 per cent of that needed for an equivalent amount of renewable energy. An added bonus for our construction companies would be that, having established CCT plants here, they would have lucrative opportunities in developing countries, where coal use is still sharply increasing. It is slightly reassuring that a parallel review of CCT is now in hand, but extremely sad that there has been fifteen years of government prevarication and no action.

Methane is twenty times more potent than carbon dioxide as a greenhouse gas. Hence another exciting development which could be linked to the regeneration of our coal industry would be to exploit various forms of methane extraction: coal mine methane (CMM), underground coal gasification (UCG) and coal bed methane (CBM). Our developments are still in their infancy, but in the USA they are already supplying 6 per cent of natural gas demands from these sources. Furthermore, carbon dioxide extracted from our power stations could be used for enhanced recovery from dormant North Sea oil wells. I believe BP set up a project team to help recover more offshore oil by extending the life of the Forties Field. An example of this process from Canada involves capturing carbon dioxide from a large coal gasification plant in the US state of North Dakota and transporting it 200 miles by pipeline to Weyburn Oilfield.

The attitude of our government to the future of nuclear energy is far from clear. In December 2001 the media reported, 'Ministers seal the fate of nuclear power stations', saying they are preparing to sound the death knell of Britain's nuclear power industry by ruling out any further tax breaks or subsidies for new reactors. The Government, however, recognizes that the nuclear option should be kept open, though current development work which could produce a new generation of reactors is fifteen to twenty years away. Currently 25 per cent of UK's electricity is generated from fifteen nuclear power stations and the oldest are seven Magnox plants. Some reactors are now approaching fifty years old, compared with the original envisaged life span of twenty-five years, and all are due to close by 2010. The seven AGR power stations are also well past their envisaged life spans of twenty-five years and again have had their lives extended by ten years, but they, too, should probably close by 2015. This would leave Sizewell B as the only remaining nuclear power station.

In Germany the position is even more critical, with the Government, urged by the Green Party, having agreed to phase out nuclear plants which currently represent nearly 30 per cent of their electricity needs. Sweden is likely to follow the same policy. The USA faces even greater nuclear power problems. The electricity consumption there is ten times more than the UK's and 20 per cent is currently nuclear based. By 2020 it is anticipated that the number of nuclear stations will be reduced from 110 to 45.

Nuclear energy faces other difficult obstacles in addition to the high cost of production. The problem of transporting and disposing of nuclear waste still remains unresolved in the eyes of the public. Thirty years ago reprocessing was adopted as government policy for dealing with spent fuel for two main reasons. Firstly, it was thought the world would run out of uranium and that reprocessing was the solution. Now we see how wrong that was; uranium is abundant and cheaper than it has ever been. Secondly, plutonium was going to be needed as the fuel of the future for the fast-breeder reactor. Wrong again, as the UK cancelled its fast-breeder reactor programme, as have most other countries. In contrast the USA went down a different route, choosing not to reprocess but to dispose of spent fuel directly. This means the fuel leaves the reactor, stays in the power station storage facility for several years and is later shipped to the national fuel repository. There it will be entombed deep underground in such a way that it will be impervious to floods and earthquakes. Compared with reprocessing, direct deposit is vastly cheaper.

I was recently invited to give evidence to the House of Lords Energy Subcommittee on future energy policy. The first question I was asked was: 'Do you think that nuclear power stations are particularly vulnerable to terrorist attacks?' I had recently returned from the USA, visiting friends near Vero Beach, where the pilots were trained who later committed the appalling atrocities of 11 September. What they said was, 'We just want you to teach us to fly, you do not need to teach us how to land planes or take off.' This, I understand, was reported to the appropriate department but apparently no meaningful action was taken. These Al-Qaida terrorists clearly accepted that if you are going to commit suicide, you might as well do it in a more dramatic way than as a traditional suicide bomber. Clearly there are terrorists who are already trained, or could be quickly trained, to follow this approach by crashing a plane on a nuclear power station and this could lead to a Chernobyl-scale explosion. We are rightly determined to hunt down countries like Iraq, who are perceived to have weapons of mass destruction like nuclear devices, but in fact every nuclear power station could be a potential hazard for our communities.

There were earlier problems I could recall because we went to live in the USA immediately after the Three Mile Island explosion. It was not a serious incident and very little radioactivity escaped outside the bounds of the plant, but it made a very deep impact on the Americans. For example, the last US power station then under construction was on Long Island and the people there just rebelled and prevented it from ever starting up. It cost about $7 billion to build and in the end was bought by the local state for $5 and, I believe, eventually replaced by a conventional power station.

It must be agreed that nuclear energy world-wide has a remarkably good safety record and I have heard many nuclear supporters rightly arguing that far more people are killed in air crashes than in nuclear accidents. However the problem with a nuclear explosion, like Chernobyl in 1986, is that it is not just confined to the people killed in the immediate explosion. There are longstanding aftereffects; we know people are still dying from this disaster and there are children who are deformed or medically ill as a result.

When I was Chairman of British Coal, there was an incident when the cooling water inlets into a French nuclear station on the River Loire froze over and no one knew immediately that it had happened. This was clearly a 'near miss', but how many such incidents have there been of which we are not aware? We only heard about this one because the French stopped delivering nuclear energy through the cross-channel link and there was a temporary surge in coal usage.

To sum up, it may be an exaggerated fear but I believe there only has to be another Chernobyl-type disaster or a nuclear power station exploded as a result of terrorist activity to put the blight yet again on any expansion of the global nuclear industry.

UK power stations are currently in rough balance between coal, gas and nuclear, but in 2025 the DTI reckons that we will have gas as the one dominating fuel – 70 per cent of the UK's electricity eggs in one basket. Our own North Sea gas production is projected to decline from 2004 and shortly after we would have to import supplies, the proportion rising to 90 per cent by 2020. Potential sources of this gas are Algeria, Iran and, mainly, Russia's Gazprom. The EU are going to be overwhelmingly dependent on Gazprom, although Algeria will supply limited quantities to Spain, Portugal and Italy. Eastern Europe, particularly Poland, are switching from coal to gas and Gazprom have growing commitments to supply China and even Japan.

Some foreseeable problems in this situation for the UK are:

- The gas would have to be delivered through pipelines thousands of miles long – across Europe and eventually piped under the Channel. We would be at the end of the pipelines and more vulnerable to any interruption.
- The pipelines would first pass through the Ukraine, which does not have an ideal relationship with its dominating neighbour.
- Pipelines are normally on the surface and impossible to protect against terrorist activity. If they wanted to disrupt energy supplies to any EU country, terrorists would be presented with the easiest possible target.
- Gazprom would probably insist on take-or-pay contracts or even on total consumption contracts.
- Gazprom could raise prices at will, as we would have no realistic bargaining chips.
- If Russia perceived that any country was behaving contrary to its political or industrial aspirations, they could easily curtail supplies as a sanction.
- The PIU report, I believe, is far too relaxed about the alternative available sources of gas because this would be a unique situation, with nearly 90 per cent of our gas coming through pipelines from Russia. There would not be any immediate alternative if this source was cut off for any of the above reasons.

I have dealt with the Russians many times in my industrial career and they are very difficult and histrionic negotiators, even in the position of buyer – and totally uncompromising when they are sellers! We can all remember the global problems constantly caused when OPEC was in its prime, but I believe that will prove to be like the proverbial tea party compared with what will happen if we place such a high dependence on Gazprom and for this reason I believe it would be a diabolical strategy.

Some positive claims of the PIU report seem to be dubious,

particularly increasing electricity generated from renewable sources to 20 per cent by 2020 and a step change in efficiency in the domestic sector of 20 per cent energy saving by 2010 plus a further 20 per cent in the following decade.

Dealing first with renewable sources. The present EU target is for these to provide 12 per cent of primary energy by 2010. However the PIU report proposes that an expanded target of 20 per cent should be set for 2020. Much of this is forecast to be produced from biomass and organic waste, with a tenfold increase in electricity generation from these fuels. To put this in perspective, the amount of biomass required, if grown as coppiced willow, would cover a land area equivalent to the combined size of Belgium, Holland and Denmark. Aspirations for wind turbines – the most promising of the renewables – are scarcely more believable. Moreover they have a serious defect: they only produce energy when the wind blows! The annual load factors of wind turbines are between 25 per cent and 30 per cent. There would be times, however, when most turbines would be operating at full load and delivering 100 per cent of their power. This maximum power output causes stability problems in the distribution networks, which would have to be modified extensively to deal with a substantial amount of wind energy. Denmark is the most developed producer with wind power accounting for about 15 per cent of their total electricity consumption, which is less than 10 per cent of the UK's. They have had serious stability problems within their electrical network. Moreover they have the highest domestic costs in Europe, more than 50 per cent higher than in the UK. Southern California has some of the largest wind farms in the world but they did not avoid serious black-outs – perhaps the right winds were not blowing!

It seems ironic, too, that proven nuclear energy will be put on hold until it can compete on equal terms with other cheaper fuels, whereas renewables under development have not very dissimilar costs and no proof of producing competitive energy without higher prices or substantial subsidies.

Having been lukewarm about the potential role of renewables, I am nevertheless surprised that the PIU report omitted to elaborate on the potential from building the Severn Barrage, which could supply 7 per cent of the UK's electricity. It is estimated that the capital cost would be about £10 billion, equivalent to, say, two nuclear plants but with a life of over 100 years. If the capital is written off over the first twenty years, the unit costs would be high but not prohibitive, and for the rest of its life it would deliver very cheap electricity at about 0.5p/kwh. Surely we can no longer ignore this potential domestic power source?

The PIU report also contains another target: a step change in domestic energy efficiency, to improve it by 20 per cent between now and 2010 and a further 20 per cent between 2010 and 2020. This would double the existing rate of improvement, which they agree is a challenging proposition.

Throughout the reports on this topic there seems to be a tendency to believe that we are faced with a fixed target of consumption, whereas demand has been rising at an annual rate of 1.5 per cent. If our manufacturing industry revives rather than declines, then the rate could be well over 2 per cent. If 2020 is the target date, then we could be faced with a potential increased demand of 40 per cent.

To sum up, the key element is that we have to ensure that we are using our domestic options to the full. Relying on importing vast quantities of gas from Russia by pipeline and raising our targets for renewables and energy saving to unachievable levels, is a recipe for disaster. Conversely I believe we have to regenerate our coal industry combined with the use of CCT, as well as exploiting the exciting new techniques of methane extraction and carbon dioxide sequestration. Also the Severn Barrage should be built.

We should view these proposals against the background of much higher international coal and gas prices, as the USA and the developing countries will burn ever-increasing quantities of fossil fuels. Since the heady 'dash for gas' days, gas prices have doubled and are likely to rise further. Hence, many UK coal mines will be able to live profitably with such enhanced price levels.

As already mentioned, I have real concerns about the potential safety hazards of nuclear energy and the disposal of nuclear waste, but the most difficult question we face at this time is whether we should accept these safety risks and maintain our nuclear capacity at least at the current level to ensure our overall self-sufficiency is great enough.

Kyoto and the Environment

I have to declare that I am a global warming sceptic. Looking back in history, you find that the hottest temperatures in the world were when dinosaurs were roaming around and I do not think anyone was producing any carbon dioxide at that time. In Roman times we had a period when temperatures were high enough in the North of England and Scotland to grow vines. Again no one was burning coal and producing carbon dioxide. Conversely,when we were burning vast quantities of coal very inefficiently, the River Thames was freezing over during the winters. The timescales of such climatic changes are very long and are almost certainly due to more natural causes like sunspot activity. Against this background, if global warming exists, it is unlikely to be sustained for ever as is threatened by the global warming fraternity. Its impact on the future will be trivial in relation to the dominating long-term natural phenomena.

In the winter of 2000/01 the UK had serious floods and the cry went out, 'There you are, that is global warming.' We were also warned that the future would herald regular annual winter floods and very hot summers. The last two summers in the UK have on the contrary been very dreary, with only the occasional really hot day. Winter flooding was undoubtedly caused by the abnormal periods of low pressure we experienced, triggered by the persistent jet streams coming across the Atlantic.

Currently the global warmers are in disarray about the cause of widespread floods in central Europe. One group claims that these are another example of global warming, in contrast to their usual claim of our summers becoming much hotter; perhaps we ought to rename the phenomenon global raining! However, other voices deny it is anything to do with global warming. They suggest that the floods originated from the Indian subcontinent during the early monsoon period. The monsoon apparently failed in July 2002 and this resulted in atypically cold and wet weather in Europe. Another outlandish possibility being posed is that the floods may be linked to El Niño – the Southern Hemisphere weather cycle developing in the Pacific Ocean! Both these phenomena are examples of natural climate patterns which have been with us for generations.

On the global scene we are constantly being told that the Arctic and Antarctic icecaps are melting rapidly and that as much as 50 per cent of the ice has now disappeared. If this has occurred, what has happened to the excess sea water? Surely parts of low-lying countries like Bangladesh would not just be exposed to occasional floods but be permanently under water. As I write, there are even claims of distinguished environmental groups having faked before and after photographs of the disappearing icecaps in the Arctic regions.

Let us assume, however, that global warming does exist as a significant factor. We have a situation now under the Kyoto Agreement where more than 50 per cent of the world is not committed – primarily the USA and most of the developing world. We have to go back to the earlier Rio Agreement, the effects of which were minimal. President Clinton went to the Senate, who indicated that the agreement could be honoured, but that any environmental measures taken must not adversely affect the US economy! That protocol, I understand, remains in force and President Bush was only being honest when he declined to sign the Kyoto Agreement. The USA might have had second thoughts on this if we Europeans had not insisted on the base date being 1990, whereas the US said that was a nonsense, it should be the Kyoto date of 1997. The Europeans, of course, were seen to be looking to capitalize on the results achieved in the intervening period, when the UK were sharply cutting back our coal industry, Germany was benefiting from reunification and the French were going nuclear.

The other problem with Kyoto is that, to get countries on board, concessions were made which left the agreement somewhat flawed – for example, trading of emissions between countries, and allowing a country to grow forests to act as a 'sink' for carbon dioxide. I believe these could prove a charter for cheats!

We obviously feel good by setting an example for others to follow. But our industry is not in such a wonderful state that we can put ourselves in an uncompetitive position with those countries who will pay only lip-service to the agreement, and not play by the rules, as we proudly will.

Relationships Between Leaders of Industry and Government Ministers and their Senior Civil Servants

When I was involved in the private sector, relations with ministers and civil servants were usually benign and helpful, with occasional clashes on a particular issue. But when you are chairman of a nationalized industry, relationships are much more intense and challenging, and on occasions quite adversarial, particularly with civil servants. The tone was usually markedly influenced by the approach of the secretary of state involved.

During my eight years chairing nationalized industries I had eight secretaries of state – although I exaggerate a little, as I had Cecil Parkinson twice, first at British Steel and then at British Coal. These rapid changes did not help to develop a continuing strategy and allowed the civil servants to create unhelpful distractions. On occasions a recently appointed secretary of state would say: 'Bob, I had a marvellous idea in the bath [or some other unlikely place] this morning.' This, needless to say, would not be the first time I had heard of this particular idea and had dismissed it – but the civil servants were determined to raise their favourite red herrings once more. It also became clear to me that civil servants did not like having a strong chairman of their industry, preferring someone who was malleable and willing to follow their line.

The secretary of state could largely establish how effective these relationships were. I used to judge them rather crudely by how often during our meetings they referred to the civil servants' brief. Peter Walker, Cecil Parkinson and Norman Tebbit hardly ever looked at the brief, whereas others would almost read it out to me!

Recognizing that both our steel and coal industries were passing through a critical time, I often wondered whether moving ministers in related government roles so frequently to meet cabinet or other political needs achieved the right balance.

Having been critical of civil servants in general, I recognize that some permanent secretaries were very helpful. Peter Gregson at the Department of Energy and Michael Franklin at the Ministry of Agriculture, when I was chairing Tate & Lyle, immediately come to mind. But the really outstanding performer in my opinion was Peter

Carey. I became acquainted with him in my ICI days and we became close friends. From time to time he sounded me out about my interest in possible government roles, including the first Chairmanship of BT. Later, as I explained in Chapter 8, he was an important influence in my appointment as Chairman of British Steel and he was also instrumental in my becoming one of the first non-executive government directors of Cable & Wireless following its privatization.

At the DTI Peter was a tower of strength. He completely immersed himself in the post and almost every evening would attend dinners or other functions with industrialists. As a result his knowledge of industry, its leaders and its problems was quite unique in my experience. He is the true role model for future generations to follow. I believe that he, too, is in the process of writing a book which should be compulsory reading for every young civil servant who is destined to work in the industrial and energy sectors.

This thought conveniently leads me back to the beginning of my book, with the real hope that my own industrial cocktail offers the present generation of business managers and those around them a lingering taste of achievements to savour as well as setbacks to avoid, as their actions steer the multitude of businesses through challenging and changing industrial times.

Acknowledgements

Acknowledgements to include copyright reprint extracts are due to the following: HarperCollins Publishers Ltd for *Scargill: The Unauthorised Biography* (1993) by Paul Routledge and for *John Major: The Autobiography* (1999); Macmillan, London, UK for *The Journals of Woodrow Wyatt*, vol. 1; Bloomsbury Publishing Ltd for *Staying Power* (1991) by Peter Walker; *Chemical Business*; *News of the World*/the late Woodrow Wyatt; and Lady Villiers for quotes from the late Sir Charles Villiers.

Index

Frame, Alistair, 99
Franklin, Michael, 184

Garnet, John, 31–2
gas production, 178–9, 181
Gazprom, 178–9
Geevor Tin Mine, Cornwall, 25
General Aniline (GAF), 47–8
George, Eddie, 169
German coal industry, 128, 175
Germany, 59–60, 75
Ghandi, Rajiv & Sonia, 71
Gibfield Colliery, 27
Gibson, Austin, 46
Glasgow, 30, 31, 32
global warming, 182–3
Goett, Ed, 78, 79
Gomia, 66, 67, 70
Goodman, Geoffrey, 125
Goodman, Louis, 56
Gormley, Joe, 116
Greenbury, Rick, 148
Gregory, Vince, 84
Gregson, John, 112
Gregson, Peter, 184
Grieves, David, 111
Grimethorpe Colliery, 128, 175
Groundnuts Scheme, 39
Gulf War, 146–7

Hale, Nathan, 81
Hall, Arnold, 86
Halstead, Ronnie, 109, 112
Hankins, Harold, 160
Hanson, Jack, 158
Harris, Martin, 160
Harrison, George, 61
Hart, David, 121
Harvey, Philip, 72
Harvey-Jones, John, 78, 86–9, 160
Haslam, Percy (father of author) 17, 18–19, 23, 53–4
Haslam, Mary-Alice (known as Cissy) (mother of author) 17, 18–19, 22, 53–4, 161
Haslam, Elizabeth (formerly Sieff, wife of author), 159, 163, 164–7
Haslam, James (grandson of author), 167
Haslam, Joyce (formerly Quin, wife of author), 27, 31, 36, 56, 60, 61, 63, 67, 70, 82, 94, 107, 114, 146, 147, 161–4

Haslam, Nigel (son of author), 162, 166, 167
Haslam, Reverend, 73
Haslam, Roberta (grand-daughter of author), 167
Haslam, Roger (son of author), 31, 161, 162, 166–7
Haslam, Sara (grand-daughter of author), 166, 167
Haslam, Sophie (grand-daughter of author), 167
'Haslam Panel', 41
'Haslam Scheme', 42
Hayes, Brian, 109
Heathfield, Peter, 119
Helsinki, University of, 60
Henderson, Denys, 66, 73
Henley Administrative Staff College (Management College), 36
Henriques, Jeffrey, 47
Heseltine, Michael, 108, 136, 137
Heseltine, Sir William, 132
Hodgson, Maurice, 72, 78, 82, 84, 85
Holm, John, 39
Hoover Dam, 142
Hopewell, Virginia, 47
Howe, Geoffrey, 170–1
HSBC, 173
Hudson, Tom, 85
Hunt, David, 115
Hunt, Kevan, 122, 140
Hurd, Douglas, 134
Hyderabad, 66, 71
Hyman, Joe, 55–7

ICI India, 38, 66–71, 72
ICI Americas, 78–86
ICI Australia, 77
ICI Fibres, 50–63
ICI Films Group, 46–9
ICI Nobel Division, 30–43
ICI Paints Division, 65, 66, 73
ICI Plastics Division, 42–50
ICI Pharmaceuticals Division, 80
India, 38, 66–8, 69–71
Industrial Society, 32
Institute of Mining Engineers, 130
Intex Yarns, 58
Iraq, 146
Ireland, 60